50 Healthy Breakfast Recipes for Home

By: Kelly Johnson

Table of Contents

- Greek Yogurt Parfait with Fresh Berries
- Overnight Oats with Chia Seeds and Almond Butter
- Avocado Toast with Tomato and Basil
- Veggie-Stuffed Egg Muffins
- Quinoa Breakfast Bowl with Spinach and Eggs
- Smoothie Bowl with Banana and Spinach
- Whole Grain Pancakes with Fresh Fruit
- Almond Flour Waffles with Greek Yogurt
- Chia Seed Pudding with Mango
- Sweet Potato Hash with Bell Peppers and Onions
- Cottage Cheese with Pineapple and Walnuts
- Oatmeal with Fresh Apples and Cinnamon
- Whole Wheat English Muffin with Avocado and Poached Egg
- Baked Banana Oatmeal Cups
- Spinach and Feta Stuffed Breakfast Wrap
- Baked Apple Cinnamon Quinoa
- Nut and Berry Granola with Almond Milk
- Veggie Omelet with Mushrooms and Bell Peppers
- Fresh Fruit Salad with Mint
- Buckwheat Pancakes with Blueberries
- Egg and Veggie Breakfast Bowl
- Almond Butter and Banana Smoothie
- Cauliflower Rice Breakfast Bowl with Eggs
- Tomato and Basil Frittata
- Apple and Cinnamon Overnight Oats
- Greek Yogurt Smoothie with Spinach and Pineapple
- Millet Porridge with Fresh Berries
- Zucchini and Carrot Breakfast Muffins
- Avocado and Tomato Breakfast Salad
- Berry and Almond Overnight Chia Pudding
- Tofu Scramble with Spinach and Tomatoes
- Oat and Nut Breakfast Bars

- Breakfast Burrito with Black Beans and Avocado
- Spiced Sweet Potato and Black Bean Breakfast Bowl
- Mango Chia Smoothie
- Quinoa and Berry Breakfast Salad
- Egg White and Veggie Breakfast Wrap
- Cottage Cheese and Berry Breakfast Bowl
- Peanut Butter and Apple Overnight Oats
- Kale and Mushroom Breakfast Frittata
- Almond Flour Banana Muffins
- Fresh Fruit and Yogurt Smoothie
- Sweet Potato and Kale Breakfast Hash
- Chia Seed and Berry Breakfast Parfait
- Spiced Pumpkin Oatmeal
- Egg and Spinach Breakfast Quesadilla
- Berry Almond Quinoa Porridge
- Whole Wheat Avocado and Egg Toast
- Spinach and Mushroom Breakfast Casserole
- Kiwi and Pineapple Chia Seed Pudding

Greek Yogurt Parfait with Fresh Berries

Ingredients:

- 1 cup Greek yogurt (plain or vanilla)
- 1/2 cup fresh strawberries, sliced
- 1/2 cup fresh blueberries
- 1/4 cup granola
- 1 tablespoon honey or maple syrup (optional)
- 1 tablespoon chia seeds (optional)
- Fresh mint leaves for garnish (optional)

Instructions:

1. **Prepare the Ingredients:**
    - Wash and slice the strawberries if needed.
    - If using, mix the chia seeds into the Greek yogurt.
2. **Assemble the Parfait:**
    - In a glass or bowl, layer half of the Greek yogurt.
    - Add a layer of fresh strawberries and blueberries.
    - Sprinkle with granola.
3. **Add More Layers:**
    - Add the remaining Greek yogurt on top of the fruit and granola.
    - Top with the remaining berries and a drizzle of honey or maple syrup if desired.
4. **Garnish:**
    - Garnish with fresh mint leaves if using.
5. **Serve:**
    - Serve immediately or refrigerate for a few hours for a chilled treat.

Enjoy your healthy and delicious Greek Yogurt Parfait!

Overnight Oats with Chia Seeds and Almond Butter

Ingredients:

- 1/2 cup rolled oats
- 1 tablespoon chia seeds
- 1 cup unsweetened almond milk (or any milk of choice)
- 1 tablespoon almond butter
- 1 tablespoon honey or maple syrup (optional)
- 1/2 teaspoon vanilla extract (optional)
- Fresh fruit, nuts, or seeds for topping (e.g., sliced bananas, berries, almonds)

Instructions:

1. **Mix the Base:**
   - In a jar or container with a lid, combine the rolled oats and chia seeds.
2. **Add Liquids:**
   - Pour in the almond milk and add the almond butter. Stir well to combine. If you're using honey or maple syrup, add it now along with the vanilla extract if desired.
3. **Stir and Combine:**
   - Stir the mixture thoroughly to ensure the almond butter is well distributed and the chia seeds are evenly mixed with the oats.
4. **Refrigerate:**
   - Cover the jar or container and refrigerate overnight (or for at least 4 hours) to allow the oats and chia seeds to absorb the liquid and soften.
5. **Add Toppings:**
   - In the morning, give the oats a good stir. Add your favorite toppings, such as fresh fruit, nuts, or additional seeds.
6. **Serve:**
   - Enjoy your overnight oats cold straight from the fridge, or warm them up if you prefer.

Feel free to adjust the sweetness and toppings to your taste. Enjoy your nutritious and easy breakfast!

Avocado Toast with Tomato and Basil

Ingredients:

- 1 ripe avocado
- 2 slices whole grain or sourdough bread
- 1 small tomato, sliced
- Fresh basil leaves
- 1 tablespoon lemon juice
- Salt and pepper to taste
- Olive oil (optional)
- Red pepper flakes (optional)

Instructions:

1. **Toast the Bread:**
   - Toast the slices of bread until they are golden brown and crispy.
2. **Prepare the Avocado:**
   - While the bread is toasting, cut the avocado in half, remove the pit, and scoop the flesh into a bowl.
   - Mash the avocado with a fork, then mix in the lemon juice, salt, and pepper.
3. **Assemble the Toast:**
   - Spread the mashed avocado evenly over the toasted bread slices.
4. **Add Tomato and Basil:**
   - Arrange the tomato slices on top of the avocado.
   - Tear fresh basil leaves and scatter them over the tomatoes.
5. **Season and Serve:**
   - Drizzle with a bit of olive oil if desired.
   - Add a pinch of red pepper flakes for a bit of heat, if you like.
   - Serve immediately.

Enjoy this fresh and flavorful avocado toast for a quick and healthy breakfast or snack!

Veggie-Stuffed Egg Muffins

Ingredients:

- 6 large eggs
- 1/4 cup milk (any kind)
- 1/2 cup diced bell peppers (any color)
- 1/2 cup chopped spinach (fresh or frozen)
- 1/4 cup finely chopped onion
- 1/4 cup shredded cheese (optional, e.g., cheddar, feta, or mozzarella)
- Salt and pepper to taste
- 1/2 teaspoon dried oregano or basil (optional)
- Cooking spray or a small amount of olive oil for greasing

Instructions:

1. **Preheat the Oven:**
    - Preheat your oven to 375°F (190°C).
2. **Prepare the Veggies:**
    - If using frozen spinach, thaw and squeeze out excess moisture.
    - Dice the bell peppers and chop the onion.
3. **Mix the Egg Base:**
    - In a large bowl, whisk together the eggs and milk. Season with salt, pepper, and dried oregano or basil if using.
4. **Add Veggies:**
    - Stir in the diced bell peppers, chopped spinach, and onion. If using cheese, add it to the mixture.
5. **Prepare Muffin Tin:**
    - Lightly grease a muffin tin with cooking spray or a small amount of olive oil. You can also use paper liners if preferred.
6. **Fill Muffin Tin:**
    - Pour the egg mixture evenly into the muffin cups, filling each about 3/4 full.
7. **Bake:**
    - Bake in the preheated oven for 20-25 minutes, or until the egg muffins are set and lightly golden on top. A toothpick inserted into the center should come out clean.
8. **Cool and Serve:**
    - Let the muffins cool in the tin for a few minutes before removing them. Serve warm or store in the refrigerator for up to a week.

Enjoy these veggie-stuffed egg muffins as a quick and nutritious breakfast or snack!

Quinoa Breakfast Bowl with Spinach and Eggs

Ingredients:

- 1 cup quinoa, rinsed
- 2 cups water or vegetable broth
- 2 cups fresh spinach (or more if desired)
- 2 large eggs
- 1 tablespoon olive oil
- Salt and pepper to taste
- 1/4 teaspoon garlic powder (optional)
- 1/4 teaspoon paprika (optional)
- Fresh herbs for garnish (optional, e.g., parsley or chives)

Instructions:

1. **Cook the Quinoa:**
   - In a medium saucepan, bring 2 cups of water or vegetable broth to a boil.
   - Add the rinsed quinoa, reduce heat to low, cover, and simmer for about 15 minutes, or until the quinoa is tender and the liquid is absorbed.
   - Fluff with a fork and set aside.
2. **Prepare the Spinach:**
   - In a large skillet, heat the olive oil over medium heat.
   - Add the fresh spinach and cook, stirring occasionally, until wilted (about 2-3 minutes). Season with a pinch of salt and pepper. Remove from heat and set aside.
3. **Cook the Eggs:**
   - In the same skillet, you can either scramble the eggs or cook them sunny-side up.
     - For scrambled eggs: Crack the eggs into a bowl, whisk them, then pour into the skillet. Cook, stirring occasionally, until fully cooked. Season with salt, pepper, garlic powder, and paprika if using.
     - For sunny-side up eggs: Crack the eggs directly into the skillet and cook until the whites are set but the yolks are still runny, about 2-3 minutes. Season with salt and pepper.
4. **Assemble the Breakfast Bowl:**
   - Divide the cooked quinoa among bowls.
   - Top with the sautéed spinach and eggs.
   - Garnish with fresh herbs if desired.
5. **Serve:**
   - Enjoy immediately while warm.

Feel free to customize this bowl with additional toppings like avocado slices, cherry tomatoes, or a sprinkle of cheese for extra flavor and nutrition.

Smoothie Bowl with Banana and Spinach

Ingredients:

- 1 large banana (preferably frozen)
- 1 cup fresh spinach (packed)
- 1/2 cup Greek yogurt (plain or vanilla)
- 1/2 cup almond milk (or any milk of choice)
- 1 tablespoon honey or maple syrup (optional)
- 1 tablespoon chia seeds (optional)
- 1/4 teaspoon vanilla extract (optional)

Toppings (optional):

- Fresh fruit (e.g., sliced banana, berries)
- Granola
- Nuts and seeds (e.g., almonds, walnuts, chia seeds)
- Coconut flakes
- Drizzle of honey or nut butter

Instructions:

1. **Blend the Smoothie:**
   - In a blender, combine the frozen banana, fresh spinach, Greek yogurt, almond milk, and honey or maple syrup (if using). Add vanilla extract if desired.
   - Blend until smooth and creamy. You may need to add a bit more milk if the mixture is too thick or blend longer to get a smoother consistency.
2. **Pour and Smooth:**
   - Pour the smoothie into a bowl and use a spoon to spread it out evenly.
3. **Add Toppings:**
   - Arrange your desired toppings over the surface of the smoothie bowl. You can get creative with the arrangement!
4. **Serve:**
   - Enjoy immediately with a spoon.

This smoothie bowl is a great way to start your day with a burst of energy and nutrients. Feel free to mix and match toppings based on your preferences!

Whole Grain Pancakes with Fresh Fruit

Ingredients:

- **For the Pancakes:**
    - 1 cup whole wheat flour
    - 1 tablespoon baking powder
    - 1/2 teaspoon salt
    - 1 cup milk (any kind, dairy or non-dairy)
    - 1 large egg
    - 2 tablespoons honey or maple syrup
    - 2 tablespoons olive oil or melted coconut oil
    - 1 teaspoon vanilla extract (optional)
- **For the Fresh Fruit Topping:**
    - 1 cup fresh fruit (e.g., berries, sliced bananas, chopped apples, or peaches)
    - 1 tablespoon honey or maple syrup (optional, for drizzling)
    - A sprinkle of cinnamon (optional)

Instructions:

1. **Prepare the Pancake Batter:**
    - In a large bowl, whisk together the whole wheat flour, baking powder, and salt.
    - In another bowl, mix the milk, egg, honey or maple syrup, olive oil or melted coconut oil, and vanilla extract (if using).
    - Pour the wet ingredients into the dry ingredients and stir until just combined. Be careful not to over-mix; a few lumps are fine.
2. **Cook the Pancakes:**
    - Heat a non-stick skillet or griddle over medium heat and lightly grease it with oil or cooking spray.
    - Pour about 1/4 cup of batter onto the skillet for each pancake. Cook until bubbles form on the surface and the edges look set, about 2-3 minutes. Flip and cook for another 1-2 minutes, or until golden brown and cooked through.
    - Transfer pancakes to a plate and keep warm. Repeat with the remaining batter.
3. **Prepare the Fresh Fruit:**
    - While the pancakes are cooking, prepare your fresh fruit. If desired, you can drizzle a little honey or maple syrup over the fruit and sprinkle with cinnamon for extra flavor.
4. **Serve:**
    - Stack the pancakes on a plate and top with the fresh fruit.
    - Serve immediately and enjoy!

These whole grain pancakes are a wholesome and satisfying breakfast option, and the fresh fruit adds a burst of natural sweetness and nutrients.

Almond Flour Waffles with Greek Yogurt

Ingredients:

- **For the Waffles:**
    - 2 cups almond flour
    - 2 large eggs
    - 1/2 cup milk (any kind, dairy or non-dairy)
    - 2 tablespoons honey or maple syrup
    - 1/4 cup melted coconut oil or butter
    - 1 teaspoon vanilla extract
    - 1 teaspoon baking powder
    - A pinch of salt
- **For Serving:**
    - 1 cup Greek yogurt (plain or vanilla)
    - Fresh fruit (e.g., berries, banana slices, or apple chunks)
    - A drizzle of honey or maple syrup (optional)
    - Nuts or seeds (optional, for added crunch)

Instructions:

1. **Preheat Waffle Iron:**
    - Preheat your waffle iron according to the manufacturer's instructions.
2. **Prepare the Waffle Batter:**
    - In a large bowl, whisk together the almond flour, baking powder, and salt.
    - In another bowl, mix the eggs, milk, honey or maple syrup, melted coconut oil or butter, and vanilla extract.
    - Pour the wet ingredients into the dry ingredients and stir until well combined.
3. **Cook the Waffles:**
    - Lightly grease the waffle iron with cooking spray or a small amount of oil.
    - Pour the batter into the preheated waffle iron, using the amount recommended by your waffle iron's instructions.
    - Close the waffle iron and cook until the waffles are golden brown and crisp. The cooking time will vary depending on your waffle iron.
4. **Serve:**
    - Remove the waffles and place them on a plate.
    - Top each waffle with a dollop of Greek yogurt and fresh fruit.
    - Drizzle with honey or maple syrup if desired, and sprinkle with nuts or seeds for added texture.

Enjoy these almond flour waffles as a delicious and healthy breakfast or brunch option!

Chia Seed Pudding with Mango

Ingredients:

- **For the Chia Seed Pudding:**
  - 1/4 cup chia seeds
  - 1 cup almond milk (or any milk of choice)
  - 1 tablespoon maple syrup or honey (optional, for sweetness)
  - 1/2 teaspoon vanilla extract (optional)
- **For the Mango Topping:**
  - 1 ripe mango, peeled and diced
  - 1 tablespoon lime juice (optional, for extra flavor)
  - Fresh mint leaves for garnish (optional)

Instructions:

1. **Prepare the Chia Seed Pudding:**
   - In a medium bowl or jar, combine the chia seeds, almond milk, maple syrup or honey, and vanilla extract if using.
   - Stir well to ensure the chia seeds are evenly distributed.
   - Cover and refrigerate for at least 4 hours, or overnight, to allow the chia seeds to absorb the liquid and thicken into a pudding-like consistency.
2. **Prepare the Mango Topping:**
   - While the pudding is setting, peel and dice the mango into small cubes.
   - If desired, toss the mango with lime juice for added flavor.
3. **Assemble the Pudding:**
   - Once the chia seed pudding has set, give it a good stir.
   - Spoon the pudding into bowls or serving glasses.
4. **Add the Toppings:**
   - Top each serving with diced mango.
   - Garnish with fresh mint leaves if using.
5. **Serve:**
   - Enjoy immediately or store in the refrigerator for up to 2 days.

This chia seed pudding with mango is a refreshing and nutritious dessert or breakfast option, providing a great combination of creamy texture and fruity sweetness.

Sweet Potato Hash with Bell Peppers and Onions

Ingredients:

- **2 medium sweet potatoes**, peeled and diced
- **1 red bell pepper**, diced
- **1 green bell pepper**, diced
- **1 medium onion**, diced
- **2 cloves garlic**, minced
- **2 tbsp olive oil** or avocado oil
- **1 tsp smoked paprika**
- **1/2 tsp ground cumin**
- **1/2 tsp dried thyme** (or a few fresh thyme leaves)
- **Salt and black pepper**, to taste
- **Optional toppings:** chopped fresh parsley, a fried egg, or avocado slices

Instructions:

1. **Prepare the Sweet Potatoes:**
   - Dice the sweet potatoes into small, even cubes. This helps them cook uniformly.
2. **Cook the Sweet Potatoes:**
   - Heat 1 tablespoon of oil in a large skillet over medium heat.
   - Add the sweet potatoes to the skillet and cook, stirring occasionally, for about 10-15 minutes, or until they start to become tender and lightly browned.
3. **Add Vegetables:**
   - Push the sweet potatoes to one side of the skillet. Add the remaining tablespoon of oil to the empty side.
   - Add the diced onion and bell peppers to the skillet. Cook for about 5 minutes, or until the vegetables start to soften.
4. **Season:**
   - Add the minced garlic, smoked paprika, cumin, thyme, salt, and black pepper.
   - Stir everything together and cook for another 5-7 minutes, or until all the vegetables are tender and the sweet potatoes are crispy and golden brown.
5. **Serve:**
   - Taste and adjust the seasoning if necessary.
   - Serve the hash hot, optionally topped with chopped fresh parsley, a fried egg, or avocado slices if you like.

Enjoy your hearty and flavorful sweet potato hash! It's great on its own or served alongside some protein like eggs or grilled chicken.

Cottage Cheese with Pineapple and Walnuts

Ingredients:

- **1 cup cottage cheese** (low-fat or full-fat, depending on preference)
- **1/2 cup fresh pineapple**, diced (or canned pineapple chunks, drained)
- **2 tbsp walnuts**, chopped (toasted if you like for extra flavor)
- **1 tbsp honey** or maple syrup (optional, for added sweetness)
- **1/4 tsp ground cinnamon** (optional, for a touch of warmth)

Instructions:

1. **Prepare Ingredients:**
   - If using fresh pineapple, peel, core, and dice it into bite-sized pieces. If using canned pineapple, ensure it's well-drained.
   - Chop the walnuts into small pieces. Toasting them in a dry pan over medium heat for a few minutes can enhance their flavor, but it's optional.
2. **Combine:**
   - In a bowl, mix the cottage cheese and pineapple together until well combined.
3. **Add Walnuts and Sweetener:**
   - Gently fold in the chopped walnuts.
   - If using, drizzle honey or maple syrup over the top and sprinkle with ground cinnamon.
4. **Serve:**
   - Serve immediately or chill in the refrigerator for a bit if you prefer it cold.

This dish is quick to make and can be customized with other fruits or nuts based on your preferences. Enjoy it as a satisfying breakfast, a snack, or even a light dessert!

Oatmeal with Fresh Apples and Cinnamon

Ingredients:

- **1 cup rolled oats**
- **2 cups water** or milk (dairy or non-dairy)
- **1 medium apple**, cored and diced (any variety you prefer)
- **1/2 tsp ground cinnamon**
- **1-2 tbsp maple syrup** or honey (to taste)
- **1/4 tsp vanilla extract** (optional)
- **Pinch of salt**
- **Optional toppings:** chopped nuts, dried fruit, or a dollop of yogurt

Instructions:

1. **Cook the Oats:**
    - In a medium saucepan, bring the water or milk to a boil.
    - Stir in the rolled oats and a pinch of salt.
    - Reduce the heat to low and simmer, stirring occasionally, for about 5 minutes, or until the oats are cooked and have absorbed most of the liquid.
2. **Add Apples and Cinnamon:**
    - While the oats are cooking, heat a small pan over medium heat. Add the diced apple and cook for 3-5 minutes, or until they start to soften.
    - Stir in the ground cinnamon and cook for an additional 1-2 minutes.
3. **Combine:**
    - Once the oats are cooked, stir in the cooked apples and cinnamon mixture.
    - Add the maple syrup or honey and vanilla extract (if using), and mix well.
4. **Serve:**
    - Spoon the oatmeal into bowls.
    - Add any additional toppings you like, such as chopped nuts, dried fruit, or a dollop of yogurt.
5. **Enjoy:**
    - Serve hot and enjoy a hearty and wholesome breakfast!

Feel free to adjust the sweetness or add extra spices to suit your taste. This recipe is versatile, so you can mix in other fruits or spices to create your perfect bowl of oatmeal.

Whole Wheat English Muffin with Avocado and Poached Egg

Ingredients:

- **1 whole wheat English muffin**
- **1 ripe avocado**
- **1 small lemon** (for juice)
- **1-2 large eggs**
- **1 tbsp white vinegar** (for poaching)
- **Salt and black pepper**, to taste
- **Optional toppings:** red pepper flakes, fresh herbs (like chives or parsley), a sprinkle of paprika

Instructions:

1. **Toast the English Muffin:**
   - Slice the whole wheat English muffin in half and toast it until golden brown. You can use a toaster or a toaster oven.
2. **Prepare the Avocado:**
   - While the muffin is toasting, cut the avocado in half, remove the pit, and scoop the flesh into a bowl.
   - Mash the avocado with a fork until smooth, or leave it a bit chunky if you prefer.
   - Squeeze in some lemon juice and season with a pinch of salt and black pepper. Mix well.
3. **Poach the Egg:**
   - Fill a small saucepan with about 2-3 inches of water and add the white vinegar. Bring the water to a gentle simmer over medium heat.
   - Crack an egg into a small bowl or ramekin. Gently slide the egg into the simmering water.
   - Use a spoon to gently swirl the water around the egg to help the white wrap around the yolk. Cook for about 3-4 minutes for a runny yolk, or a bit longer if you prefer a firmer yolk.
   - Carefully remove the egg with a slotted spoon and place it on a paper towel to drain.
4. **Assemble the Muffin:**
   - Spread the mashed avocado evenly over the toasted English muffin halves.
   - Top each muffin half with a poached egg.
   - Season with additional salt and pepper, and add optional toppings like red pepper flakes, fresh herbs, or paprika.
5. **Serve:**
   - Serve immediately while the egg is warm and the avocado is creamy.

This simple yet satisfying dish provides a great balance of healthy fats, protein, and whole grains. It's perfect for a quick, nutritious meal!

Baked Banana Oatmeal Cups

Ingredients:

- **2 ripe bananas**, mashed
- **1 1/2 cups rolled oats**
- **1/2 cup milk** (dairy or non-dairy)
- **1/4 cup honey** or maple syrup (adjust to taste)
- **1/4 cup nut butter** (like almond or peanut butter, optional for extra creaminess)
- **1 tsp vanilla extract**
- **1/2 tsp ground cinnamon**
- **1/2 tsp baking powder**
- **1/4 tsp salt**
- **1/4 cup raisins** or chocolate chips (optional)
- **1/4 cup chopped nuts** (optional, for added crunch)

Instructions:

1. **Preheat Oven:**
   - Preheat your oven to 350°F (175°C) and line a muffin tin with paper liners or lightly grease it.
2. **Mix Ingredients:**
   - In a large bowl, combine the mashed bananas, rolled oats, milk, honey or maple syrup, nut butter (if using), vanilla extract, ground cinnamon, baking powder, and salt. Stir until well combined.
   - If you're adding raisins, chocolate chips, or nuts, fold them into the mixture.
3. **Fill Muffin Tin:**
   - Divide the mixture evenly among the muffin cups, filling each about 3/4 full.
4. **Bake:**
   - Bake in the preheated oven for 20-25 minutes, or until the tops are golden brown and a toothpick inserted into the center comes out clean.
5. **Cool:**
   - Allow the oatmeal cups to cool in the tin for about 5 minutes before transferring them to a wire rack to cool completely.
6. **Serve:**
   - Enjoy them warm or at room temperature. They can be stored in an airtight container at room temperature for a couple of days or refrigerated for up to a week. You can also freeze them for longer storage; just reheat in the microwave or oven before eating.

Tips:

- **Customization:** Feel free to add other mix-ins like chopped dried fruit, seeds (chia or flax), or fresh berries.
- **Sweetness:** Adjust the amount of sweetener according to the ripeness of your bananas and personal taste preferences.

These baked oatmeal cups are not only delicious but also nutritious, making them a great choice for a quick and satisfying meal!

Spinach and Feta Stuffed Breakfast Wrap

Ingredients:

- **1 large whole wheat tortilla** (or your preferred type)
- **2 large eggs**
- **1 cup fresh spinach**, chopped
- **1/4 cup feta cheese**, crumbled
- **1/4 cup diced onion** (optional)
- **1/4 cup diced bell pepper** (optional)
- **1 tbsp olive oil** or butter
- **Salt and black pepper**, to taste
- **Optional add-ins:** cherry tomatoes, mushrooms, fresh herbs (like chives or parsley)

Instructions:

1. **Prepare the Vegetables:**
   - Heat the olive oil or butter in a skillet over medium heat.
   - If using onion and bell pepper, add them to the skillet and cook until softened, about 3-4 minutes.
2. **Cook the Spinach:**
   - Add the chopped spinach to the skillet and cook until wilted, about 1-2 minutes. Season with a pinch of salt and pepper. Remove from the skillet and set aside.
3. **Scramble the Eggs:**
   - In a bowl, whisk the eggs with a pinch of salt and pepper.
   - Pour the eggs into the skillet and scramble, cooking until just set.
4. **Combine Ingredients:**
   - Add the cooked spinach mixture and crumbled feta cheese to the scrambled eggs. Stir gently to combine.
5. **Assemble the Wrap:**
   - Warm the tortilla in a dry skillet over medium heat or microwave for about 10-15 seconds until pliable.
   - Spoon the egg and spinach mixture onto the center of the tortilla.
6. **Wrap and Cook:**
   - Fold in the sides of the tortilla and then roll it up from the bottom, enclosing the filling.
   - If desired, you can toast the wrap in a skillet over medium heat, seam side down, for a minute or so to seal it and add a bit of crispiness.
7. **Serve:**
   - Slice the wrap in half if you like and serve hot.

Tips:

- **Customization:** Feel free to add other ingredients like cooked bacon, avocado slices, or fresh herbs for extra flavor.
- **Make Ahead:** You can prepare the filling in advance and store it in the refrigerator. Reheat and assemble the wrap when ready to eat.

This Spinach and Feta Stuffed Breakfast Wrap is a great way to start your day with a nutritious meal that's both satisfying and easy to make!

Baked Apple Cinnamon Quinoa

Ingredients:

- **1 cup quinoa**
- **2 cups water** or unsweetened almond milk (for a creamier texture)
- **2 medium apples**, peeled, cored, and diced
- **1/4 cup maple syrup** or honey (adjust to taste)
- **1 tsp ground cinnamon**
- **1/2 tsp ground nutmeg** (optional)
- **1/4 cup raisins** or dried cranberries (optional)
- **1/4 cup chopped nuts** (e.g., walnuts, pecans, optional)
- **1/2 tsp vanilla extract** (optional)
- **Pinch of salt**

Instructions:

1. **Preheat Oven:**
   - Preheat your oven to 350°F (175°C). Grease or lightly coat a baking dish (an 8x8 inch dish works well) with non-stick spray or oil.
2. **Cook Quinoa:**
   - Rinse the quinoa under cold water.
   - In a medium saucepan, bring 2 cups of water or almond milk to a boil.
   - Add the quinoa and a pinch of salt. Reduce heat to low, cover, and simmer for about 15 minutes, or until the quinoa is cooked and the liquid is absorbed. Fluff with a fork.
3. **Prepare Apple Mixture:**
   - In a large bowl, combine the diced apples, maple syrup or honey, ground cinnamon, and nutmeg (if using). Toss to coat the apples evenly.
4. **Combine and Bake:**
   - In the same bowl, mix the cooked quinoa with the apple mixture. If you're adding raisins, dried cranberries, or nuts, fold them in at this stage.
   - Stir in the vanilla extract, if using.
5. **Transfer to Baking Dish:**
   - Transfer the mixture to the prepared baking dish and spread it out evenly.
6. **Bake:**
   - Bake in the preheated oven for 25-30 minutes, or until the apples are tender and the top is slightly golden.
7. **Cool and Serve:**
   - Let the dish cool slightly before serving. It can be enjoyed warm or at room temperature.

Tips:

- **Customization:** Feel free to add other fruits like berries or pears, or mix in some chia seeds or flaxseeds for extra nutrition.
- **Storage:** Leftovers can be stored in an airtight container in the refrigerator for up to a week. It also freezes well; just reheat it in the microwave or oven.

This Baked Apple Cinnamon Quinoa is a wholesome, versatile dish that can be enjoyed in various ways, making it a great addition to your meal planning.

Nut and Berry Granola with Almond Milk

Ingredients:

- **3 cups old-fashioned rolled oats**
- **1 cup mixed nuts** (e.g., almonds, walnuts, pecans), chopped
- **1/2 cup sunflower seeds** or pumpkin seeds
- **1/2 cup shredded coconut** (optional)
- **1/2 cup honey** or maple syrup
- **1/4 cup coconut oil** or olive oil
- **1 tsp vanilla extract**
- **1/2 tsp ground cinnamon**
- **1/4 tsp salt**
- **1 cup dried mixed berries** (e.g., cranberries, blueberries, raisins)

Instructions:

1. **Preheat Oven:**
    - Preheat your oven to 325°F (163°C) and line a baking sheet with parchment paper.
2. **Mix Dry Ingredients:**
    - In a large bowl, combine the rolled oats, chopped nuts, sunflower seeds, and shredded coconut (if using).
3. **Prepare Wet Ingredients:**
    - In a small saucepan, heat the honey or maple syrup and coconut oil over low heat until melted and combined. Stir in the vanilla extract.
4. **Combine and Coat:**
    - Pour the wet mixture over the dry ingredients and stir until everything is evenly coated.
5. **Bake:**
    - Spread the granola mixture in an even layer on the prepared baking sheet.
    - Bake for 20-25 minutes, stirring once halfway through, until the granola is golden brown and fragrant.
6. **Add Berries:**
    - Remove from the oven and let it cool completely on the baking sheet. Once cooled, stir in the dried berries.
7. **Store:**
    - Store the granola in an airtight container at room temperature for up to two weeks.

Serving with Almond Milk

1. **Prepare the Almond Milk:**

- Pour almond milk into a bowl. Use unsweetened almond milk for a lower sugar option, or flavored almond milk if you prefer a bit of extra sweetness.
2. **Add Granola:**
    - Spoon a serving of granola into the bowl with the almond milk.
3. **Optional Toppings:**
    - Add fresh fruit, such as sliced bananas, berries, or a drizzle of honey for added flavor if desired.
4. **Enjoy:**
    - Enjoy immediately as a crunchy, creamy breakfast or snack.

Tips:

- **Customization:** Feel free to adjust the nuts and seeds based on your preferences. You can also add other mix-ins like coconut flakes, chia seeds, or flaxseeds.
- **Sweetness:** Adjust the amount of honey or maple syrup according to your taste preferences.

This Nut and Berry Granola with Almond Milk is a versatile and wholesome option that's perfect for busy mornings or a satisfying snack!

Veggie Omelet with Mushrooms and Bell Peppers

Ingredients:

- **3 large eggs**
- **1/4 cup milk** (dairy or non-dairy)
- **1/2 cup mushrooms**, sliced
- **1/2 cup bell peppers**, diced (any color or a mix)
- **1/4 cup onion**, diced (optional)
- **1 tbsp olive oil** or butter
- **Salt and black pepper**, to taste
- **1/4 cup shredded cheese** (optional, e.g., cheddar, feta, or mozzarella)
- **Fresh herbs** (e.g., chives, parsley) for garnish (optional)

Instructions:

1. **Prepare the Vegetables:**
    - Heat the olive oil or butter in a non-stick skillet over medium heat.
    - Add the diced onion (if using) and cook for 1-2 minutes until softened.
    - Add the sliced mushrooms and bell peppers. Cook for about 5-7 minutes, stirring occasionally, until the mushrooms are golden and the peppers are tender. Season with a pinch of salt and pepper. Remove from the skillet and set aside.
2. **Prepare the Egg Mixture:**
    - In a bowl, whisk together the eggs, milk, salt, and pepper until well combined.
3. **Cook the Omelet:**
    - In the same skillet, add a little more olive oil or butter if needed and heat over medium-low heat.
    - Pour the egg mixture into the skillet, tilting the pan to spread the eggs evenly.
    - Let the eggs cook undisturbed for about 1-2 minutes until the edges start to set.
4. **Add the Vegetables:**
    - Once the eggs are mostly set but still slightly runny on top, spread the cooked vegetables evenly over one half of the omelet.
    - Sprinkle the shredded cheese on top of the vegetables if using.
5. **Fold and Finish:**
    - Carefully fold the other half of the omelet over the filling to create a half-moon shape.
    - Cook for another 1-2 minutes, or until the eggs are fully set and the cheese is melted (if using).
6. **Serve:**
    - Slide the omelet onto a plate and garnish with fresh herbs if desired.
    - Serve hot.

Tips:

- **Customization:** Feel free to add other veggies like spinach, tomatoes, or zucchini, or even proteins like cooked bacon or sausage for extra flavor.
- **Seasoning:** Experiment with different seasonings or herbs to customize the flavor.

This Veggie Omelet with Mushrooms and Bell Peppers is not only delicious but also versatile and packed with nutrients. It's perfect for a quick, satisfying breakfast or a light meal at any time of day!

Fresh Fruit Salad with Mint

Ingredients:

- **2 cups strawberries**, hulled and sliced
- **2 cups blueberries**
- **2 cups watermelon**, cubed
- **1 cup mango**, peeled and cubed
- **1 cup kiwi**, peeled and sliced
- **1/2 cup fresh mint leaves**, finely chopped
- **1-2 tbsp honey** or agave syrup (optional, for added sweetness)
- **Juice of 1 lime** (optional, for added zing)

Instructions:

1. **Prepare the Fruit:**
   - Wash and prepare all the fruit as indicated. Hull and slice the strawberries, peel and cube the mango, peel and slice the kiwi, and cube the watermelon.
2. **Mix the Fruit:**
   - In a large bowl, combine the strawberries, blueberries, watermelon, mango, and kiwi.
3. **Add Mint:**
   - Finely chop the fresh mint leaves and add them to the bowl of fruit.
4. **Sweeten and Season:**
   - If desired, drizzle honey or agave syrup over the fruit for added sweetness.
   - Squeeze the lime juice over the fruit for a bit of tanginess (optional).
5. **Toss and Chill:**
   - Gently toss the fruit salad to combine all ingredients.
   - Chill in the refrigerator for at least 30 minutes before serving to allow the flavors to meld.
6. **Serve:**
   - Serve the fruit salad chilled. Garnish with a few additional mint leaves if desired.

Tips:

- **Customization:** Feel free to use any seasonal fruit or berries you like. You can also add other fruits such as pineapple, peaches, or grapes.
- **Make Ahead:** This fruit salad can be made a few hours in advance, but it's best enjoyed fresh. The mint can lose its flavor over time, so add it just before serving if you're preparing it earlier.

This Fresh Fruit Salad with Mint is not only delicious and refreshing but also packed with vitamins and antioxidants, making it a perfect choice for a healthy and tasty treat!

Buckwheat Pancakes with Blueberries

Ingredients:

For the Pancakes:

- **1 cup buckwheat flour**
- **1 cup all-purpose flour** (or use all buckwheat flour for gluten-free)
- **2 tbsp sugar** (or sweetener of your choice)
- **2 tsp baking powder**
- **1/2 tsp baking soda**
- **1/2 tsp salt**
- **1 1/2 cups buttermilk** (or use milk with 1 tbsp lemon juice or vinegar)
- **2 large eggs**
- **1/4 cup melted butter** or vegetable oil
- **1 tsp vanilla extract** (optional)

For the Blueberries:

- **1 cup fresh or frozen blueberries**
- **1 tbsp sugar** (optional, for extra sweetness)
- **1 tsp lemon juice** (optional)

Instructions:

1. **Prepare the Blueberries:**
    - In a small saucepan over medium heat, combine the blueberries, sugar (if using), and lemon juice (if using). Cook for about 5 minutes, or until the blueberries are softened and the sauce is slightly thickened. Set aside.
2. **Prepare the Pancake Batter:**
    - In a large bowl, whisk together the buckwheat flour, all-purpose flour, sugar, baking powder, baking soda, and salt.
    - In another bowl, whisk together the buttermilk, eggs, melted butter, and vanilla extract.
    - Pour the wet ingredients into the dry ingredients and stir until just combined. The batter will be slightly lumpy, which is okay.
3. **Cook the Pancakes:**
    - Heat a non-stick skillet or griddle over medium heat. Lightly grease with butter or oil.
    - Pour about 1/4 cup of batter onto the skillet for each pancake. Cook until bubbles form on the surface and the edges start to look set, about 2-3 minutes. Flip and cook for another 1-2 minutes, or until golden brown and cooked through.
    - Keep cooked pancakes warm in a low oven while you cook the remaining pancakes.

4. **Serve:**
    - Serve the pancakes warm with the blueberry topping spooned over the top. You can also add a drizzle of maple syrup if desired.

Tips:

- **Customization:** Feel free to add other mix-ins like chocolate chips or nuts to the batter before cooking.
- **Make Ahead:** Pancakes can be made in advance and reheated in a toaster or oven. They also freeze well; just layer with parchment paper and store in a freezer bag.

These Buckwheat Pancakes with Blueberries offer a wholesome twist on a classic breakfast and are sure to please both gluten-free and non-gluten-free eaters alike!

Egg and Veggie Breakfast Bowl

Ingredients:

- **2 large eggs**
- **1 cup cooked quinoa** or brown rice (for a base; optional)
- **1 cup fresh spinach** or kale, chopped
- **1/2 cup bell peppers**, diced
- **1/2 cup cherry tomatoes**, halved
- **1/4 cup red onion**, diced
- **1/2 avocado**, sliced
- **1 tbsp olive oil**
- **Salt and black pepper**, to taste
- **1/4 tsp paprika** (optional)
- **1/4 tsp garlic powder** (optional)
- **1/4 tsp dried herbs** (e.g., thyme, oregano; optional)
- **Fresh herbs** for garnish (e.g., parsley, chives; optional)
- **Hot sauce** or **salsa** for serving (optional)

Instructions:

1. **Prepare the Base (if using):**
   - If you're using quinoa or brown rice, cook according to package instructions and set aside.
2. **Cook the Vegetables:**
   - Heat the olive oil in a skillet over medium heat.
   - Add the diced red onion and cook for 2-3 minutes until softened.
   - Add the bell peppers and cook for another 3-4 minutes, until they start to soften.
   - Stir in the cherry tomatoes and cook for 1-2 minutes until slightly softened.
   - Add the spinach or kale and cook until wilted, about 1-2 minutes. Season with salt, black pepper, paprika, garlic powder, and dried herbs (if using). Remove from heat.
3. **Cook the Eggs:**
   - In a separate skillet, heat a little oil or butter over medium-low heat.
   - Crack the eggs into the skillet and cook to your desired doneness (sunny-side up, over-easy, or scrambled). Season with salt and pepper.
4. **Assemble the Bowl:**
   - If using a base like quinoa or brown rice, place a serving in the bottom of your bowl.
   - Top with the cooked vegetables.
   - Add the cooked eggs on top.
   - Arrange avocado slices around the eggs.
5. **Serve:**

- Garnish with fresh herbs if desired.
- Add hot sauce or salsa on the side for extra flavor if you like.

Tips:

- **Customization:** Feel free to add other veggies such as mushrooms, zucchini, or sweet potatoes. You can also include proteins like cooked chicken or beans.
- **Meal Prep:** This breakfast bowl can be prepped in advance. Store the cooked veggies and base separately from the eggs and avocado. Assemble and heat when ready to eat.
- **Variations:** Experiment with different seasonings or cheese like feta or shredded cheddar for added flavor.

This Egg and Veggie Breakfast Bowl is not only delicious but also packed with nutrients, making it a great choice for a healthy and satisfying start to your day!

Almond Butter and Banana Smoothie

Ingredients:

- **1 large banana**, peeled and sliced (fresh or frozen)
- **2 tbsp almond butter**
- **1 cup milk** (dairy or non-dairy, like almond milk, oat milk, or soy milk)
- **1/2 cup Greek yogurt** (plain or vanilla, for extra creaminess and protein)
- **1 tbsp honey** or maple syrup (optional, for added sweetness)
- **1/2 tsp vanilla extract** (optional)
- **1/4 tsp ground cinnamon** (optional)
- **Ice cubes** (optional, for a thicker smoothie)

Instructions:

1. **Combine Ingredients:**
   - In a blender, combine the banana, almond butter, milk, Greek yogurt, honey or maple syrup (if using), vanilla extract (if using), and ground cinnamon (if using).
2. **Blend:**
   - Blend until smooth and creamy. If you prefer a thicker smoothie, add a handful of ice cubes and blend again until well combined.
3. **Taste and Adjust:**
   - Taste the smoothie and adjust sweetness if needed. You can add more honey or maple syrup if you like it sweeter.
4. **Serve:**
   - Pour the smoothie into a glass and serve immediately. You can also garnish with a sprinkle of cinnamon or a few banana slices on top if desired.

Tips:

- **Frozen Banana:** Using a frozen banana will make the smoothie thicker and colder. If you don't have frozen bananas, you can use fresh and add ice cubes.
- **Protein Boost:** For an extra protein boost, consider adding a scoop of protein powder or chia seeds.
- **Flavor Variations:** Experiment with adding other ingredients like spinach for a green smoothie, or a tablespoon of cocoa powder for a chocolate twist.

This Almond Butter and Banana Smoothie is a great way to enjoy a quick, nutritious, and satisfying drink that's both delicious and easy to make!

Cauliflower Rice Breakfast Bowl with Eggs

Ingredients:

For the Cauliflower Rice:

- **1 head of cauliflower**, or about 4 cups cauliflower rice (store-bought or homemade)
- **1 tbsp olive oil**
- **1/2 cup onion**, diced
- **1 cup bell peppers**, diced
- **1 cup spinach** or kale, chopped
- **1/2 tsp garlic powder** (optional)
- **Salt and black pepper**, to taste

For the Eggs:

- **2 large eggs**
- **1 tbsp butter** or oil (for cooking eggs)
- **Salt and black pepper**, to taste

Optional Toppings:

- **Avocado slices**
- **Cherry tomatoes**, halved
- **Fresh herbs** (e.g., parsley, chives)
- **Sriracha** or hot sauce
- **Shredded cheese** (e.g., cheddar, feta)

Instructions:

1. **Prepare the Cauliflower Rice:**
    - **Homemade Cauliflower Rice:** Remove the leaves and stem from the cauliflower. Cut it into florets and pulse in a food processor until it resembles rice grains. If you don't have a food processor, you can grate the cauliflower using a box grater.
    - **Cook the Cauliflower Rice:** Heat the olive oil in a large skillet over medium heat. Add the diced onion and cook until softened, about 3-4 minutes.
    - Add the bell peppers and cook for another 3 minutes.
    - Stir in the cauliflower rice and cook for about 5-7 minutes, stirring occasionally, until the cauliflower is tender and slightly golden. Add the spinach or kale and cook until wilted. Season with garlic powder (if using), salt, and pepper. Remove from heat and set aside.
2. **Cook the Eggs:**
    - Heat butter or oil in a non-stick skillet over medium heat.

- Crack the eggs into the skillet and cook to your desired doneness (sunny-side up, over-easy, or scrambled). Season with salt and pepper.
3. **Assemble the Breakfast Bowl:**
    - Divide the cauliflower rice mixture between bowls.
    - Top each bowl with a cooked egg.
    - Add optional toppings like avocado slices, cherry tomatoes, fresh herbs, hot sauce, or shredded cheese.
4. **Serve:**
    - Serve immediately and enjoy a nutritious and satisfying breakfast bowl!

Tips:

- **Customization:** Feel free to add other veggies or proteins, such as cooked chicken or beans, to the cauliflower rice for extra variety.
- **Meal Prep:** You can make the cauliflower rice ahead of time and store it in the refrigerator for up to 4 days. Reheat before serving.

This Cauliflower Rice Breakfast Bowl with Eggs is a great way to enjoy a healthy, low-carb breakfast that's both delicious and satisfying!

Tomato and Basil Frittata

Ingredients:

- **6 large eggs**
- **1/4 cup milk** (dairy or non-dairy)
- **1 cup cherry tomatoes**, halved (or 1 large tomato, diced)
- **1/2 cup fresh basil leaves**, chopped (or 1-2 tbsp dried basil)
- **1/2 cup shredded cheese** (e.g., mozzarella, feta, or cheddar; optional)
- **1/2 cup onion**, diced (optional)
- **1 garlic clove**, minced (optional)
- **1 tbsp olive oil**
- **Salt and black pepper**, to taste
- **1/4 tsp dried oregano** (optional)

Instructions:

1. **Preheat Oven:**
    - Preheat your oven to 375°F (190°C). If you don't have an oven-safe skillet, you can use a regular skillet and transfer to a baking dish later.
2. **Prepare the Vegetables:**
    - Heat the olive oil in an oven-safe skillet over medium heat.
    - Add the diced onion (if using) and cook until softened, about 3-4 minutes.
    - Add the minced garlic (if using) and cook for an additional 30 seconds until fragrant.
    - Add the cherry tomatoes and cook for 2-3 minutes until they start to soften. Season with a pinch of salt and pepper. Remove from heat.
3. **Prepare the Egg Mixture:**
    - In a large bowl, whisk together the eggs, milk, and a pinch of salt and pepper. Stir in the chopped basil and shredded cheese (if using).
4. **Combine and Cook:**
    - Pour the egg mixture over the cooked vegetables in the skillet. Stir gently to combine.
    - Cook on the stovetop over medium heat for about 2-3 minutes, or until the edges start to set.
5. **Transfer to Oven:**
    - Transfer the skillet to the preheated oven and bake for 15-20 minutes, or until the frittata is fully set and the top is golden brown.
6. **Cool and Serve:**
    - Let the frittata cool slightly before slicing. Garnish with extra fresh basil if desired.

Tips:

- **Customization:** Feel free to add other ingredients such as cooked bacon, ham, or additional vegetables like bell peppers or spinach.
- **Make Ahead:** The frittata can be made ahead of time and stored in the refrigerator for up to 4 days. It can also be frozen for longer storage. Reheat in the microwave or oven before serving.

This Tomato and Basil Frittata is a simple yet elegant dish that's sure to be a hit at any meal!

Apple and Cinnamon Overnight Oats

Ingredients:

- **1 cup rolled oats**
- **1 cup milk** (dairy or non-dairy, such as almond milk or oat milk)
- **1/2 cup plain Greek yogurt** (for added creaminess and protein; optional)
- **1 medium apple**, peeled, cored, and diced
- **1 tbsp maple syrup** or honey (adjust to taste)
- **1 tsp ground cinnamon**
- **1/4 tsp ground nutmeg** (optional)
- **1/4 tsp vanilla extract** (optional)
- **2 tbsp chia seeds** (optional, for added texture and nutrition)
- **1/4 cup nuts** (e.g., walnuts or almonds, chopped; optional)
- **1/4 cup raisins** or dried cranberries (optional)

Instructions:

1. **Prepare the Base:**
   - In a large bowl, combine the rolled oats, milk, and Greek yogurt (if using).
2. **Add Flavorings:**
   - Stir in the maple syrup or honey, ground cinnamon, and ground nutmeg (if using). Mix well to combine.
3. **Add Apple:**
   - Gently fold in the diced apple.
4. **Add Optional Ingredients:**
   - If using chia seeds, nuts, or dried fruit, stir them into the mixture.
5. **Refrigerate:**
   - Cover the bowl with a lid or plastic wrap and refrigerate overnight (or for at least 6 hours) to allow the oats to soak and absorb the flavors.
6. **Serve:**
   - In the morning, give the oats a good stir. If the mixture is too thick, you can add a little more milk to reach your desired consistency.
   - Top with additional fresh apple slices, a sprinkle of cinnamon, or a drizzle of honey or maple syrup if desired.

Tips:

- **Customization:** Feel free to adjust the sweetness and spices according to your taste. You can also add other mix-ins like fresh berries, nuts, or seeds.
- **Texture:** For a creamier texture, increase the amount of Greek yogurt or use a bit of mashed banana in place of some of the milk.

- **Meal Prep:** You can make a batch of these overnight oats and store individual servings in jars or containers for up to 5 days in the refrigerator.

Apple and Cinnamon Overnight Oats are a delightful way to enjoy a wholesome breakfast that's ready to go when you are!

Greek Yogurt Smoothie with Spinach and Pineapple

Ingredients:

- **1 cup Greek yogurt** (plain or vanilla)
- **1 cup fresh spinach** (packed)
- **1 cup pineapple chunks** (fresh or frozen)
- **1 banana** (fresh or frozen, for added creaminess and sweetness)
- **1/2 cup almond milk** or other milk of your choice (adjust for desired consistency)
- **1 tbsp honey** or maple syrup (optional, for extra sweetness)
- **1/2 tsp chia seeds** or flaxseeds (optional, for added nutrition)

Instructions:

1. **Prepare Ingredients:**
    - If using fresh pineapple, cut it into chunks. If using frozen pineapple, you can skip adding ice to the smoothie.
    - Peel and slice the banana.
2. **Blend:**
    - In a blender, combine the Greek yogurt, spinach, pineapple chunks, banana, and almond milk.
    - Blend until smooth. If the smoothie is too thick, add a bit more milk to reach your desired consistency.
3. **Add Sweetener (if needed):**
    - Taste the smoothie and add honey or maple syrup if you prefer it sweeter. Blend again to mix in the sweetener.
4. **Optional Boost:**
    - If using chia seeds or flaxseeds, add them to the blender and pulse a few times to incorporate.
5. **Serve:**
    - Pour the smoothie into a glass and enjoy immediately.

Tips:

- **Customization:** You can add other fruits like mango or berries for a different flavor profile. You can also include a handful of oats for extra fiber.
- **Texture:** For a thicker smoothie, use frozen pineapple and banana. For a lighter smoothie, use fresh fruit and add a handful of ice cubes.
- **Make Ahead:** If you're short on time, you can prepare the ingredients the night before and blend them in the morning. Alternatively, you can freeze the smoothie in portions for a quick grab-and-go option.

This Greek Yogurt Smoothie with Spinach and Pineapple is not only delicious but also packed with vitamins, minerals, and protein, making it a great addition to a healthy diet!

Millet Porridge with Fresh Berries

Ingredients:

- **1 cup millet**
- **2 cups water** or **milk** (dairy or non-dairy)
- **1/4 tsp salt**
- **1 tbsp honey** or maple syrup (optional, for sweetness)
- **1/2 tsp vanilla extract** (optional)
- **1 cup fresh berries** (e.g., strawberries, blueberries, raspberries)
- **1/4 cup nuts** (e.g., almonds, walnuts), chopped (optional)
- **1/4 cup Greek yogurt** (optional, for creaminess)
- **1/2 tsp ground cinnamon** (optional)

Instructions:

1. **Rinse and Toast the Millet:**
   - Rinse the millet under cold water to remove any dust or debris.
   - In a dry skillet over medium heat, toast the millet for about 3-4 minutes, stirring frequently until it starts to emit a nutty aroma. This step adds extra flavor but can be skipped if you're in a hurry.
2. **Cook the Millet:**
   - In a medium saucepan, bring the water or milk to a boil. Add a pinch of salt.
   - Stir in the millet, reduce heat to low, and cover.
   - Simmer for about 15-20 minutes, or until the millet is tender and the liquid is absorbed. Stir occasionally to prevent sticking.
3. **Add Flavorings:**
   - Once the millet is cooked, stir in the honey or maple syrup (if using) and vanilla extract (if using). For a bit of spice, you can also add ground cinnamon.
4. **Serve:**
   - Spoon the millet porridge into bowls.
   - Top with fresh berries, chopped nuts (if using), and a dollop of Greek yogurt (if using).
   - Sprinkle with additional cinnamon if desired.
5. **Enjoy:**
   - Serve warm and enjoy a hearty, satisfying breakfast.

Tips:

- **Customizations:** You can mix in other fruits, such as sliced bananas or apples, or add seeds like chia or flax for added nutrition.
- **Make Ahead:** Millet porridge can be made ahead of time and stored in the refrigerator for up to 5 days. Reheat with a splash of milk or water to loosen it up.

- **Texture:** Adjust the thickness of the porridge by adding more or less liquid based on your preference.

This Millet Porridge with Fresh Berries is a great way to start your day with a hearty, wholesome meal that's both satisfying and packed with nutrients!

Zucchini and Carrot Breakfast Muffins

Ingredients:

- **1 cup whole wheat flour** (or all-purpose flour)
- **1/2 cup rolled oats**
- **1/2 tsp baking powder**
- **1/2 tsp baking soda**
- **1/2 tsp ground cinnamon**
- **1/4 tsp ground nutmeg** (optional)
- **1/4 tsp salt**
- **1/2 cup brown sugar** or coconut sugar (adjust to taste)
- **1/4 cup honey** or maple syrup
- **1/4 cup coconut oil** or vegetable oil, melted
- **2 large eggs**
- **1 tsp vanilla extract**
- **1 cup zucchini**, grated and excess moisture squeezed out
- **1/2 cup carrot**, grated
- **1/4 cup chopped nuts** (e.g., walnuts or pecans; optional)
- **1/4 cup raisins** or dried cranberries (optional)

Instructions:

1. **Preheat Oven:**
   - Preheat your oven to 350°F (175°C). Line a muffin tin with paper liners or lightly grease it.
2. **Prepare Dry Ingredients:**
   - In a large bowl, whisk together the flour, rolled oats, baking powder, baking soda, cinnamon, nutmeg (if using), and salt.
3. **Prepare Wet Ingredients:**
   - In another bowl, whisk together the brown sugar, honey or maple syrup, melted coconut oil or vegetable oil, eggs, and vanilla extract.
4. **Combine Wet and Dry Ingredients:**
   - Pour the wet ingredients into the dry ingredients and stir until just combined.
   - Fold in the grated zucchini and carrot. If using nuts and raisins or dried cranberries, fold them in as well.
5. **Fill Muffin Tin:**
   - Divide the batter evenly among the muffin cups, filling each about 2/3 full.
6. **Bake:**
   - Bake in the preheated oven for 18-22 minutes, or until a toothpick inserted into the center comes out clean and the tops are golden brown.
7. **Cool:**

- Let the muffins cool in the tin for about 5 minutes, then transfer to a wire rack to cool completely.
8. **Serve:**
   - Enjoy the muffins warm or at room temperature. They make a great on-the-go breakfast or snack!

Tips:

- **Customization:** Feel free to add other mix-ins like shredded coconut, chocolate chips, or seeds.
- **Storage:** Store muffins in an airtight container at room temperature for up to 3 days, or freeze for up to 3 months. Reheat in the microwave or toaster oven before serving.
- **Moisture:** Make sure to squeeze out as much moisture as possible from the grated zucchini to avoid soggy muffins.

These Zucchini and Carrot Breakfast Muffins are a tasty and nutritious way to start your day or enjoy as a mid-day snack. They are packed with fiber and vitamins and can easily be adapted to suit your taste!

Avocado and Tomato Breakfast Salad

Ingredients:

- **1 ripe avocado**, peeled, pitted, and diced
- **1 cup cherry tomatoes**, halved (or 1 large tomato, diced)
- **1/4 red onion**, finely diced
- **1/4 cucumber**, diced (optional)
- **1-2 cups mixed greens** (e.g., spinach, arugula, or lettuce; optional)
- **1 tbsp olive oil**
- **1 tbsp lemon juice** or balsamic vinegar
- **Salt and black pepper**, to taste
- **1/4 tsp dried oregano** or fresh basil (optional)
- **1/4 cup crumbled feta cheese** or goat cheese (optional)
- **1 hard-boiled egg**, sliced (optional, for extra protein)

Instructions:

1. **Prepare the Vegetables:**
   - In a large bowl, combine the diced avocado, cherry tomatoes, red onion, and cucumber (if using).
2. **Make the Dressing:**
   - In a small bowl, whisk together the olive oil and lemon juice or balsamic vinegar. Season with salt, black pepper, and dried oregano or fresh basil (if using).
3. **Assemble the Salad:**
   - Drizzle the dressing over the avocado and tomato mixture. Toss gently to combine, making sure the ingredients are evenly coated.
4. **Add Optional Ingredients:**
   - If using, add the crumbled feta cheese or goat cheese and sliced hard-boiled egg. Gently toss again.
5. **Serve:**
   - If using mixed greens, place them on a serving plate or bowl and top with the avocado and tomato mixture. Alternatively, serve the salad as is.
6. **Enjoy:**
   - Serve immediately for the freshest taste, or refrigerate for up to an hour before serving.

Tips:

- **Customization:** Feel free to add other ingredients such as olives, capers, or a sprinkle of nuts or seeds for added texture and flavor.

- **Avocado:** To prevent the avocado from browning, toss the salad just before serving. If preparing in advance, store the avocado and dressing separately and combine them right before eating.
- **Protein Boost:** To make the salad more filling, you can add grilled chicken, chickpeas, or quinoa.

This Avocado and Tomato Breakfast Salad is a great way to start your day with a burst of fresh flavors and nutrients!

Berry and Almond Overnight Chia Pudding

Ingredients:

- **1/4 cup chia seeds**
- **1 cup almond milk** (or other milk of your choice)
- **1 tbsp maple syrup** or honey (adjust to taste)
- **1/2 tsp vanilla extract** (optional)
- **1/2 cup mixed berries** (fresh or frozen; e.g., strawberries, blueberries, raspberries)
- **2 tbsp sliced almonds** (for topping)
- **1/4 cup Greek yogurt** (optional, for added creaminess)
- **1/2 tsp ground cinnamon** (optional)

Instructions:

1. **Prepare the Chia Pudding:**
   - In a medium bowl or jar, combine the chia seeds, almond milk, maple syrup (or honey), and vanilla extract (if using). Stir well to mix.
   - Let the mixture sit for about 5 minutes, then stir again to prevent the chia seeds from clumping together.
2. **Refrigerate:**
   - Cover the bowl or jar with a lid or plastic wrap. Refrigerate overnight, or for at least 4 hours, to allow the chia seeds to absorb the liquid and form a pudding-like texture.
3. **Prepare the Berries:**
   - If using frozen berries, thaw them slightly before using. You can also lightly mash them if you prefer a more jam-like consistency.
4. **Assemble the Pudding:**
   - Once the chia pudding has set, give it a good stir to ensure it's evenly mixed.
   - Spoon the pudding into serving bowls or jars.
5. **Add Toppings:**
   - Top the chia pudding with mixed berries, sliced almonds, and a dollop of Greek yogurt (if using). Sprinkle with ground cinnamon if desired.
6. **Serve:**
   - Enjoy the pudding immediately, or store it in the refrigerator for up to 3 days. It makes a great grab-and-go breakfast or snack!

Tips:

- **Customization:** Feel free to mix in other fruits like banana slices or apple chunks, or add a spoonful of nut butter for extra flavor and nutrition.
- **Texture:** If you prefer a smoother texture, you can blend the chia pudding before serving. If you like it thicker, reduce the amount of milk slightly.

- **Sweetness:** Adjust the level of sweetness according to your taste. You can also use other sweeteners like agave syrup or stevia if preferred.

Berry and Almond Overnight Chia Pudding is a delicious and versatile way to enjoy a healthy breakfast that's ready when you are!

Tofu Scramble with Spinach and Tomatoes

Ingredients:

- **1 block (14 oz) firm or extra-firm tofu**, drained and crumbled
- **1 tbsp olive oil** or cooking oil of choice
- **1/2 cup onion**, diced
- **2 cloves garlic**, minced
- **1 cup cherry tomatoes**, halved (or 1 large tomato, diced)
- **2 cups fresh spinach** (or other leafy greens)
- **1/2 tsp turmeric** (for color and flavor)
- **1/2 tsp smoked paprika** (optional, for a smoky flavor)
- **Salt and black pepper**, to taste
- **1/4 tsp cumin** (optional)
- **Fresh herbs** (e.g., parsley or chives) for garnish

Instructions:

1. **Prepare the Tofu:**
   - Drain the tofu and pat it dry with paper towels. Crumble it into small pieces resembling scrambled eggs.
2. **Cook the Aromatics:**
   - Heat the olive oil in a large skillet over medium heat. Add the diced onion and cook until softened and translucent, about 3-4 minutes.
   - Add the minced garlic and cook for an additional 30 seconds, or until fragrant.
3. **Add the Tofu:**
   - Add the crumbled tofu to the skillet. Cook, stirring occasionally, for about 5 minutes until the tofu starts to brown slightly.
4. **Season and Add Vegetables:**
   - Stir in the turmeric, smoked paprika (if using), cumin (if using), salt, and black pepper. Mix well to coat the tofu with the spices.
   - Add the cherry tomatoes and cook for another 3-4 minutes until they start to soften.
5. **Add the Spinach:**
   - Stir in the fresh spinach and cook until wilted, about 1-2 minutes. Taste and adjust seasoning if needed.
6. **Serve:**
   - Garnish with fresh herbs if desired. Serve the tofu scramble warm, either on its own or with toast, avocado, or your favorite breakfast sides.

Tips:

- **Texture:** For a firmer texture, use extra-firm tofu and press out as much moisture as possible before cooking.
- **Customization:** Feel free to add other vegetables like bell peppers, mushrooms, or zucchini. You can also mix in some nutritional yeast for a cheesy flavor.
- **Storage:** Store leftovers in an airtight container in the refrigerator for up to 3 days. Reheat in a skillet or microwave before serving.

This Tofu Scramble with Spinach and Tomatoes is a versatile and nutritious breakfast that can be enjoyed any day of the week. It's easy to prepare, full of flavor, and packed with plant-based goodness!

Oat and Nut Breakfast Bars

Ingredients:

- **2 cups rolled oats**
- **1/2 cup nuts** (e.g., almonds, walnuts, pecans), chopped
- **1/2 cup dried fruit** (e.g., raisins, cranberries, apricots), chopped
- **1/4 cup honey** or maple syrup
- **1/4 cup natural nut butter** (e.g., almond butter, peanut butter)
- **1/4 cup almond flour** or whole wheat flour (optional, for extra texture)
- **1/4 tsp vanilla extract** (optional)
- **1/4 tsp salt**
- **1/2 tsp ground cinnamon** (optional)

Instructions:

1. **Preheat Oven:**
    - Preheat your oven to 350°F (175°C). Line an 8x8 inch baking pan with parchment paper or lightly grease it.
2. **Mix Dry Ingredients:**
    - In a large bowl, combine the rolled oats, chopped nuts, chopped dried fruit, salt, and ground cinnamon (if using).
3. **Prepare Wet Ingredients:**
    - In a small saucepan over low heat, warm the honey (or maple syrup) and nut butter until they are melted and well combined. Remove from heat and stir in the vanilla extract (if using).
4. **Combine and Mix:**
    - Pour the wet mixture over the dry ingredients and mix well until everything is evenly coated.
5. **Press into Pan:**
    - Transfer the mixture to the prepared baking pan. Use a spatula or the back of a spoon to press the mixture firmly and evenly into the pan.
6. **Bake:**
    - Bake in the preheated oven for 15-20 minutes, or until the edges are golden brown and the center is set.
7. **Cool and Slice:**
    - Let the bars cool in the pan for about 10 minutes, then lift them out using the parchment paper and transfer to a wire rack to cool completely. Once cooled, cut into squares or rectangles.
8. **Store:**
    - Store the bars in an airtight container at room temperature for up to 1 week, or in the refrigerator for up to 2 weeks. You can also freeze them for longer storage.

Tips:

- **Customization:** Feel free to mix and match your favorite nuts and dried fruits. You can also add seeds (like chia or flaxseeds) or chocolate chips for extra flavor.
- **Texture:** For a chewier texture, add extra nut butter. For a firmer texture, use less nut butter or add a bit more flour.
- **Sweetness:** Adjust the amount of honey or maple syrup based on your sweetness preference.

These Oat and Nut Breakfast Bars are a delicious, healthy, and convenient option for busy mornings or as a satisfying snack any time of day. Enjoy!

Breakfast Burrito with Black Beans and Avocado

Ingredients:

- **1 large flour tortilla** (or whole wheat, spinach, or gluten-free)
- **1/2 cup black beans**, drained and rinsed
- **1/2 avocado**, sliced
- **2 large eggs**
- **1/4 cup shredded cheese** (e.g., cheddar, Monterey Jack; optional)
- **1/4 cup salsa** or diced tomatoes
- **1/4 cup fresh cilantro**, chopped (optional)
- **1 tbsp olive oil** or cooking oil
- **Salt and black pepper**, to taste
- **1/4 tsp ground cumin** (optional)
- **1/4 tsp paprika** (optional)

Instructions:

1. **Prepare the Ingredients:**
   - If you haven't already, slice the avocado and chop the fresh cilantro (if using).
   - Heat the black beans in a small saucepan over low heat, adding a pinch of salt and pepper if desired.
2. **Cook the Eggs:**
   - In a bowl, whisk the eggs with a pinch of salt, black pepper, and optional ground cumin and paprika.
   - Heat the olive oil in a non-stick skillet over medium heat.
   - Pour the eggs into the skillet and cook, stirring gently, until they are scrambled and just set. Remove from heat.
3. **Assemble the Burrito:**
   - Warm the tortilla in a dry skillet over medium heat for about 30 seconds on each side, or microwave for about 15 seconds, to make it more pliable.
   - Lay the tortilla flat on a plate.
   - Spread the cooked scrambled eggs evenly down the center of the tortilla.
   - Top with black beans, avocado slices, shredded cheese (if using), salsa, and fresh cilantro.
4. **Wrap the Burrito:**
   - Fold in the sides of the tortilla and then roll it up from the bottom, tucking in the filling as you go to ensure everything stays inside.
5. **Serve:**
   - Cut the burrito in half if desired, and serve warm.

Tips:

- **Customization:** Feel free to add other ingredients like sautéed onions, bell peppers, spinach, or mushrooms for extra flavor and nutrition.
- **Spice:** Add hot sauce or a sprinkle of chili flakes if you like a bit of heat.
- **Meal Prep:** You can prepare the filling in advance and store it in the refrigerator for up to 3 days. Simply reheat and assemble the burritos when ready to eat. You can also freeze individual burritos for up to 3 months. Wrap them tightly in foil or plastic wrap before freezing, and reheat in the microwave or oven.

This Breakfast Burrito with Black Beans and Avocado is a hearty, tasty, and versatile meal that will keep you satisfied throughout your morning!

Spiced Sweet Potato and Black Bean Breakfast Bowl

Ingredients:

- **1 large sweet potato**, peeled and diced
- **1 tbsp olive oil**
- **1/2 tsp ground cumin**
- **1/2 tsp smoked paprika**
- **1/4 tsp ground cinnamon** (optional)
- **Salt and black pepper**, to taste
- **1 cup black beans**, drained and rinsed (canned or cooked)
- **1/2 avocado**, sliced
- **1/4 cup diced red onion**
- **1/4 cup chopped fresh cilantro** (optional)
- **1/4 cup crumbled feta cheese** or cotija cheese (optional)
- **1 lime**, cut into wedges (for serving)
- **1/4 cup salsa** or diced tomatoes (optional)
- **1/4 tsp chili powder** or cayenne pepper (optional, for extra heat)

Instructions:

1. **Preheat Oven:**
   - Preheat your oven to 425°F (220°C).
2. **Prepare Sweet Potatoes:**
   - In a large bowl, toss the diced sweet potatoes with olive oil, ground cumin, smoked paprika, ground cinnamon (if using), salt, and black pepper until well coated.
3. **Roast Sweet Potatoes:**
   - Spread the seasoned sweet potatoes in a single layer on a baking sheet.
   - Roast in the preheated oven for 20-25 minutes, or until tender and slightly crispy, flipping halfway through.
4. **Heat Black Beans:**
   - While the sweet potatoes are roasting, heat the black beans in a small saucepan over medium heat until warmed through. Season with a pinch of salt and pepper.
5. **Assemble the Bowl:**
   - Once the sweet potatoes are roasted, divide them among serving bowls.
   - Top with black beans, avocado slices, diced red onion, and crumbled cheese (if using).
6. **Add Toppings:**
   - Garnish with fresh cilantro (if using), a squeeze of lime juice, and salsa or diced tomatoes (if desired). Sprinkle with chili powder or cayenne pepper for extra heat if you like.
7. **Serve:**

- Serve warm and enjoy!

Tips:

- **Customization:** You can add other vegetables like sautéed bell peppers, spinach, or kale for extra nutrition. You can also mix in cooked quinoa or brown rice for additional texture and protein.
- **Meal Prep:** The sweet potatoes and black beans can be cooked ahead of time and stored in the refrigerator for up to 4 days. Assemble the bowls when ready to eat.
- **Spice Level:** Adjust the amount of spices and chili powder according to your taste preference.

This Spiced Sweet Potato and Black Bean Breakfast Bowl is a versatile and satisfying meal that provides a great balance of flavors and nutrients to start your day right!

Mango Chia Smoothie

Ingredients:

- **1 cup fresh or frozen mango chunks**
- **1/2 cup Greek yogurt** (plain or vanilla) or a non-dairy alternative
- **1/2 cup almond milk** or other milk of your choice (adjust for desired consistency)
- **1 tbsp chia seeds**
- **1-2 tbsp honey** or maple syrup (optional, for extra sweetness)
- **1/2 tsp vanilla extract** (optional)
- **1/2 cup spinach** (optional, for added nutrients and a green boost)
- **Ice cubes** (optional, if using fresh mango and you prefer a colder smoothie)

Instructions:

1. **Prepare Chia Seeds:**
   - If you have time, soak the chia seeds in 1/4 cup of water or milk for about 10 minutes to let them expand and become gel-like. This step is optional but helps achieve a smoother texture.
2. **Blend Ingredients:**
   - In a blender, combine the mango chunks, Greek yogurt, almond milk, and soaked chia seeds (if pre-soaked). If you're using spinach or ice cubes, add them to the blender as well.
3. **Sweeten:**
   - Add honey or maple syrup to taste, depending on your preference for sweetness. If using vanilla extract, add it now.
4. **Blend:**
   - Blend until smooth and creamy. If the smoothie is too thick, add a little more almond milk to reach your desired consistency.
5. **Serve:**
   - Pour the smoothie into a glass and enjoy immediately.

Tips:

- **Customization:** Feel free to add other fruits like bananas or berries for different flavors. You can also mix in a handful of oats or protein powder for added texture and nutrition.
- **Frozen Mango:** Using frozen mango will make the smoothie thicker and colder. If you're using fresh mango, you might want to add a few ice cubes to achieve a similar texture.
- **Chia Seeds:** If you don't have time to soak the chia seeds, you can still add them directly to the blender. They will blend in, but the smoothie might be slightly less smooth.

This Mango Chia Smoothie is a delightful and wholesome drink that's not only tasty but also packed with vitamins, minerals, and healthy fats. Enjoy it as a quick breakfast or a refreshing snack!

Quinoa and Berry Breakfast Salad

Ingredients:

- **1 cup quinoa**, rinsed
- **2 cups water** or low-sodium vegetable broth (for cooking quinoa)
- **1 cup mixed berries** (e.g., strawberries, blueberries, raspberries)
- **1/4 cup chopped nuts** (e.g., almonds, walnuts, pecans)
- **2 tbsp honey** or maple syrup
- **1 tbsp lemon juice**
- **1 tbsp olive oil**
- **1/4 tsp vanilla extract** (optional)
- **Fresh mint or basil leaves** (optional, for garnish)

Instructions:

1. **Cook the Quinoa:**
    - In a medium saucepan, bring 2 cups of water or vegetable broth to a boil. Add the rinsed quinoa, reduce the heat to low, and cover.
    - Simmer for about 15 minutes, or until the quinoa is cooked and the liquid is absorbed. Remove from heat and let it sit, covered, for 5 minutes. Fluff with a fork and allow it to cool to room temperature.
2. **Prepare the Dressing:**
    - In a small bowl, whisk together the honey (or maple syrup), lemon juice, olive oil, and vanilla extract (if using). Adjust sweetness and acidity to taste.
3. **Assemble the Salad:**
    - In a large bowl, combine the cooked quinoa, mixed berries, and chopped nuts.
    - Pour the dressing over the salad and gently toss to combine.
4. **Serve:**
    - Garnish with fresh mint or basil leaves if desired.
    - Serve immediately or chill in the refrigerator for about 30 minutes before serving.

Tips:

- **Customizations:** Feel free to add other ingredients such as shredded coconut, chia seeds, or a sprinkle of feta cheese for added flavor and texture.
- **Berry Options:** You can use fresh or frozen berries. If using frozen, make sure they are thawed and drained before adding to the salad.
- **Make-Ahead:** This salad can be made ahead and stored in the refrigerator for up to 3 days. The flavors will meld together as it sits.

This Quinoa and Berry Breakfast Salad is a delightful mix of textures and flavors, making it a perfect option for a wholesome start to your day!

Egg White and Veggie Breakfast Wrap

Ingredients:

- **3-4 egg whites**
- **1 tbsp olive oil** or cooking spray
- **1/2 cup bell peppers**, diced (any color)
- **1/2 cup spinach** or kale, chopped
- **1/4 cup onion**, finely diced
- **1/4 cup tomatoes**, diced
- **1/4 cup shredded cheese** (optional, e.g., cheddar, feta, or mozzarella)
- **1 whole wheat or flour tortilla**
- **Salt and black pepper**, to taste
- **1/4 tsp paprika** or ground cumin (optional, for extra flavor)
- **1 tbsp fresh herbs** (e.g., chives, parsley), chopped (optional)

Instructions:

1. **Prepare the Vegetables:**
    - Heat the olive oil in a non-stick skillet over medium heat. Add the diced onion and bell peppers. Sauté for 3-4 minutes until they start to soften.
    - Add the chopped spinach (or kale) and tomatoes. Cook for another 1-2 minutes until the spinach is wilted and the tomatoes are slightly softened. Season with salt, black pepper, and paprika or ground cumin (if using). Remove from heat.
2. **Cook the Egg Whites:**
    - In a bowl, whisk the egg whites with a pinch of salt and pepper.
    - In the same skillet, add a bit more oil or cooking spray if needed, and pour in the egg whites. Cook over medium heat, gently stirring until they are fully cooked and set, about 2-3 minutes.
3. **Assemble the Wrap:**
    - Lay the tortilla flat on a plate. Sprinkle with shredded cheese if using.
    - Spread the cooked veggies evenly over one half of the tortilla.
    - Spoon the scrambled egg whites on top of the veggies.
4. **Wrap It Up:**
    - Fold in the sides of the tortilla and then roll it up from the bottom to secure the filling inside.
5. **Serve:**
    - If desired, heat the wrap in the skillet for 1-2 minutes on each side, or in a sandwich press, until the tortilla is crispy and the cheese is melted.
    - Slice in half and enjoy warm!

Tips:

- **Customizations:** Add other vegetables like mushrooms, zucchini, or avocado. You can also incorporate cooked beans or a spread like hummus for extra protein and flavor.
- **Make-Ahead:** You can prepare the veggie mixture and cook the egg whites ahead of time. Store them separately in the refrigerator and assemble the wraps when ready to eat.
- **Extras:** Top your wrap with salsa, hot sauce, or a dollop of Greek yogurt for additional flavor.

This Egg White and Veggie Breakfast Wrap is a versatile, nutritious, and satisfying meal that's perfect for busy mornings or a quick lunch!

Cottage Cheese and Berry Breakfast Bowl

Ingredients:

- **1 cup cottage cheese** (low-fat or full-fat, depending on your preference)
- **1/2 cup mixed berries** (e.g., strawberries, blueberries, raspberries)
- **1-2 tbsp honey** or maple syrup (optional, for extra sweetness)
- **1 tbsp chia seeds** (optional, for added fiber and omega-3s)
- **1-2 tbsp sliced almonds** or other nuts (optional, for crunch)
- **1 tbsp granola** or oatmeal (optional, for added texture)
- **Fresh mint leaves** (optional, for garnish)

Instructions:

1. **Prepare the Berries:**
   - If using fresh berries, rinse them under cold water and pat dry. If using frozen berries, thaw them slightly before using.
2. **Assemble the Bowl:**
   - Scoop the cottage cheese into a serving bowl.
3. **Add Toppings:**
   - Top the cottage cheese with mixed berries.
   - Drizzle with honey or maple syrup if you like a bit of extra sweetness.
   - Sprinkle chia seeds, sliced almonds, and granola over the top if using.
4. **Garnish:**
   - Garnish with fresh mint leaves for a touch of freshness.
5. **Serve:**
   - Enjoy immediately, or cover and store in the refrigerator for up to 1 day.

Tips:

- **Customization:** Feel free to adjust the type and amount of berries based on your preference or what's in season. You can also add other fruits like banana slices or apple chunks.
- **Texture:** For extra crunch, try adding a spoonful of your favorite granola or a handful of nuts. For a creamier texture, mix in a bit of Greek yogurt.
- **Sweetness:** Adjust the level of sweetness based on your taste. You can also use natural sweeteners like agave syrup or stevia.

This Cottage Cheese and Berry Breakfast Bowl is not only easy to prepare but also provides a balanced mix of protein, fiber, and healthy fats to keep you energized throughout the morning. Enjoy!

Peanut Butter and Apple Overnight Oats

Ingredients:

- **1/2 cup rolled oats**
- **1/2 cup milk** (dairy or non-dairy, like almond milk)
- **1/4 cup plain Greek yogurt** (optional, for extra creaminess)
- **1 tbsp peanut butter** (or almond butter)
- **1 small apple**, diced
- **1 tbsp chia seeds** (optional, for added fiber and omega-3s)
- **1-2 tbsp honey** or maple syrup (optional, for added sweetness)
- **1/2 tsp ground cinnamon** (optional, for extra flavor)
- **A pinch of salt**
- **Sliced almonds** or **granola** (for topping, optional)

Instructions:

1. **Combine Ingredients:**
   - In a jar or container with a lid, combine the rolled oats, milk, Greek yogurt (if using), and chia seeds (if using). Stir to mix well.
2. **Add Peanut Butter:**
   - Add the peanut butter and mix until well incorporated. It's okay if the peanut butter doesn't completely dissolve; it will blend in as it sits.
3. **Sweeten and Flavor:**
   - Stir in the honey or maple syrup, ground cinnamon, and a pinch of salt.
4. **Add Apples:**
   - Fold in the diced apple, or you can save the apple to add fresh in the morning if you prefer a bit more crunch.
5. **Refrigerate:**
   - Cover the jar or container with a lid and refrigerate overnight, or for at least 4 hours.
6. **Serve:**
   - In the morning, give the oats a good stir. Add a splash of milk if needed to reach your desired consistency.
   - Top with sliced almonds, granola, or extra apple slices if desired.

Tips:

- **Customization:** Feel free to add other mix-ins like raisins, dried cranberries, or a sprinkle of nuts for extra texture and flavor.
- **Apple Prep:** To prevent the apples from browning, you can toss them with a little lemon juice before adding them to the oats, or add them fresh in the morning.

- **Peanut Butter Alternatives:** If you have a nut allergy or prefer a different flavor, you can use sunflower seed butter or cashew butter instead of peanut butter.

These Peanut Butter and Apple Overnight Oats are a quick, easy, and satisfying breakfast that will keep you full and energized throughout the morning. Enjoy!

Kale and Mushroom Breakfast Frittata

Ingredients:

- **1 tbsp olive oil**
- **1 cup mushrooms**, sliced (e.g., cremini, button, or shiitake)
- **1 cup kale**, chopped (stems removed)
- **1/2 cup onion**, diced
- **3-4 large eggs**
- **1/4 cup milk** (dairy or non-dairy)
- **1/2 cup shredded cheese** (optional, e.g., cheddar, feta, or goat cheese)
- **Salt and black pepper**, to taste
- **1/4 tsp garlic powder** (optional)
- **1/4 tsp paprika** (optional)
- **Fresh herbs** (e.g., parsley, chives) for garnish (optional)

Instructions:

1. **Preheat Oven:**
   - Preheat your oven to 375°F (190°C).
2. **Sauté Vegetables:**
   - Heat the olive oil in an oven-safe skillet (preferably non-stick or cast iron) over medium heat.
   - Add the diced onion and cook until softened, about 3 minutes.
   - Add the sliced mushrooms and cook for another 5 minutes, or until they are browned and tender.
   - Add the chopped kale and cook for 2-3 minutes, or until it's wilted. Season with salt and pepper.
3. **Prepare the Egg Mixture:**
   - In a bowl, whisk together the eggs, milk, garlic powder (if using), paprika (if using), and a pinch more salt and pepper.
4. **Combine and Cook:**
   - Pour the egg mixture over the sautéed vegetables in the skillet. Stir gently to distribute the vegetables evenly in the egg mixture.
   - If using cheese, sprinkle it evenly over the top.
5. **Bake:**
   - Transfer the skillet to the preheated oven and bake for 20-25 minutes, or until the frittata is set in the center and the top is lightly golden. A toothpick or knife inserted into the center should come out clean.
6. **Cool and Serve:**
   - Let the frittata cool slightly before slicing. Garnish with fresh herbs if desired.
   - Serve warm or at room temperature.

Tips:

- **Vegetable Variations:** You can customize this frittata with other vegetables such as bell peppers, zucchini, or tomatoes. Just be sure to cook them first to remove excess moisture.
- **Cheese Options:** Feel free to use your favorite cheese or omit it for a dairy-free version.
- **Make-Ahead:** This frittata can be made ahead of time and stored in the refrigerator for up to 4 days. It can be enjoyed cold or reheated.

This Kale and Mushroom Breakfast Frittata is a flavorful and hearty dish that's perfect for busy mornings or leisurely brunches. Enjoy!

Almond Flour Banana Muffins

Ingredients:

- **2 ripe bananas**, mashed
- **1 1/2 cups almond flour**
- **1/4 cup honey** or maple syrup
- **3 large eggs**
- **1/4 cup coconut oil** or melted butter
- **1 tsp baking powder**
- **1/2 tsp baking soda**
- **1/2 tsp ground cinnamon** (optional)
- **1/4 tsp salt**
- **1/2 tsp vanilla extract** (optional)
- **1/4 cup chopped nuts** (optional, e.g., walnuts or pecans)
- **1/4 cup chocolate chips** (optional)

Instructions:

1. **Preheat Oven:**
    - Preheat your oven to 350°F (175°C). Line a muffin tin with paper liners or lightly grease the cups.
2. **Mix Wet Ingredients:**
    - In a large bowl, whisk together the mashed bananas, honey (or maple syrup), eggs, and melted coconut oil (or butter) until well combined.
3. **Combine Dry Ingredients:**
    - In another bowl, mix the almond flour, baking powder, baking soda, ground cinnamon (if using), and salt.
4. **Combine Wet and Dry Ingredients:**
    - Gradually add the dry ingredients to the wet ingredients, stirring until just combined. Be careful not to overmix.
    - If desired, fold in the chopped nuts and/or chocolate chips.
5. **Fill Muffin Tin:**
    - Divide the batter evenly among the muffin cups, filling each about 3/4 full.
6. **Bake:**
    - Bake in the preheated oven for 20-25 minutes, or until a toothpick inserted into the center of a muffin comes out clean.
7. **Cool:**
    - Allow the muffins to cool in the tin for about 5 minutes, then transfer them to a wire rack to cool completely.

Tips:

- **Ripeness:** Use very ripe bananas for the best sweetness and flavor.
- **Storage:** Store the muffins in an airtight container at room temperature for up to 3 days, or in the refrigerator for up to 1 week. They can also be frozen for up to 3 months. To freeze, wrap individually and place in a freezer-safe bag.
- **Add-Ins:** Feel free to customize the muffins with other add-ins such as dried fruit, seeds, or spices like nutmeg or cardamom.

These Almond Flour Banana Muffins are a tasty and wholesome treat that makes for a great breakfast or snack. Enjoy!

Fresh Fruit and Yogurt Smoothie

Ingredients:

- **1 cup fresh fruit** (e.g., berries, mango, pineapple, banana, or a combination)
- **1/2 cup Greek yogurt** (plain or vanilla) or any other yogurt of your choice
- **1/2 cup milk** (dairy or non-dairy, like almond milk) or more for desired consistency
- **1-2 tbsp honey** or maple syrup (optional, for added sweetness)
- **1 tbsp chia seeds** or flaxseeds (optional, for added fiber and omega-3s)
- **1/2 tsp vanilla extract** (optional)
- **A few ice cubes** (optional, for a colder smoothie)

Instructions:

1. **Prepare the Fruit:**
   - Wash and chop the fresh fruit as needed. If using a fruit like banana, you can simply peel and slice it.
2. **Blend Ingredients:**
   - In a blender, combine the fresh fruit, Greek yogurt, and milk. Add honey or maple syrup if you prefer a sweeter smoothie. For extra nutrition, add chia seeds or flaxseeds.
3. **Add Vanilla:**
   - Add vanilla extract if using, for extra flavor.
4. **Blend Until Smooth:**
   - Blend on high until the mixture is smooth and creamy. If the smoothie is too thick, add a little more milk to reach your desired consistency. If using ice cubes, add them and blend again until well combined.
5. **Serve:**
   - Pour the smoothie into glasses and serve immediately. You can also garnish with a few fresh fruit pieces or a sprinkle of granola if desired.

Tips:

- **Fruit Options:** Use a mix of your favorite fruits or what's in season. Frozen fruits can be used as a substitute for fresh fruit if you prefer a thicker smoothie.
- **Yogurt Alternatives:** If you prefer a dairy-free smoothie, you can use coconut yogurt, almond milk yogurt, or any other non-dairy yogurt.
- **Sweetness:** Adjust the sweetness to your taste by adding more or less honey/maple syrup. You can also use a ripe banana to naturally sweeten the smoothie.

This Fresh Fruit and Yogurt Smoothie is a delicious and easy way to get your daily dose of fruit and protein. Enjoy!

Sweet Potato and Kale Breakfast Hash

Ingredients:

- **1 large sweet potato**, peeled and diced
- **1 tbsp olive oil** or avocado oil
- **1 small onion**, diced
- **1 bell pepper**, diced (any color)
- **2-3 cloves garlic**, minced
- **2 cups kale**, stems removed and chopped
- **1/2 tsp smoked paprika**
- **1/2 tsp ground cumin**
- **1/4 tsp ground turmeric** (optional, for color and flavor)
- **Salt and black pepper**, to taste
- **2-3 large eggs** (optional, for topping)
- **Fresh herbs** (e.g., parsley, cilantro) for garnish (optional)

Instructions:

1. **Prepare Sweet Potatoes:**
   - Heat olive oil in a large skillet over medium heat. Add the diced sweet potatoes and cook, stirring occasionally, for about 10 minutes, or until they start to soften.
2. **Add Vegetables:**
   - Add the diced onion and bell pepper to the skillet. Continue to cook for another 5-7 minutes, or until the vegetables are tender and the sweet potatoes are cooked through. Stir occasionally.
3. **Add Garlic and Spices:**
   - Add the minced garlic, smoked paprika, ground cumin, ground turmeric (if using), salt, and black pepper. Stir well and cook for another 1-2 minutes until the garlic is fragrant and the spices are well distributed.
4. **Incorporate Kale:**
   - Add the chopped kale to the skillet. Cook for another 2-3 minutes, or until the kale is wilted and tender. Stir to combine everything thoroughly.
5. **Optional Egg Topping:**
   - If you're adding eggs, you can either cook them separately or make space in the hash for them. To cook eggs in the hash, create small wells in the mixture and crack the eggs into these wells. Cover the skillet with a lid and cook over low heat until the eggs are set to your liking (about 5-7 minutes).
6. **Serve:**
   - Transfer the hash to plates or bowls. Garnish with fresh herbs if desired.

Tips:

- **Customization:** Feel free to add other vegetables like mushrooms, zucchini, or spinach based on your preference or what you have on hand.
- **Spice Level:** Adjust the spices according to your taste. For a bit of heat, you can add a pinch of cayenne pepper or red pepper flakes.
- **Storage:** Leftovers can be stored in an airtight container in the refrigerator for up to 4 days. Reheat in the skillet or microwave before serving.

This Sweet Potato and Kale Breakfast Hash is a nutritious and satisfying way to kickstart your day, providing a balanced mix of carbs, protein, and greens. Enjoy!

Chia Seed and Berry Breakfast Parfait

Ingredients:

For the Chia Seed Pudding:

- **1/4 cup chia seeds**
- **1 cup milk** (dairy or non-dairy, like almond milk)
- **1-2 tbsp honey** or maple syrup (optional, for sweetness)
- **1/2 tsp vanilla extract** (optional)

For the Parfait:

- **1 cup mixed fresh berries** (e.g., strawberries, blueberries, raspberries)
- **1/4 cup granola** (for topping, optional)
- **Fresh mint leaves** (for garnish, optional)

Instructions:

1. **Prepare Chia Seed Pudding:**
   - In a bowl or jar, mix the chia seeds with the milk, honey (or maple syrup), and vanilla extract. Stir well to combine.
   - Cover and refrigerate for at least 4 hours or overnight. The chia seeds will absorb the liquid and expand, creating a pudding-like consistency. Stir occasionally to ensure the seeds are evenly distributed and not clumping together.
2. **Prepare the Berries:**
   - Wash and slice the berries if necessary. If using strawberries, you can slice them into smaller pieces.
3. **Assemble the Parfait:**
   - In serving glasses or bowls, start by layering a portion of chia seed pudding at the bottom.
   - Add a layer of fresh berries on top of the chia pudding.
   - Repeat the layers until you reach the top of the glass or bowl.
   - Top with a sprinkle of granola for added crunch.
4. **Garnish and Serve:**
   - Garnish with fresh mint leaves if desired.
   - Serve immediately or chill in the refrigerator until ready to eat.

Tips:

- **Sweetness:** Adjust the sweetness of the chia pudding to your taste. You can also use a flavored yogurt or milk if you prefer a different flavor profile.
- **Add-Ins:** Feel free to mix in other ingredients such as nuts, seeds, or shredded coconut into the chia pudding for added texture and nutrition.

- **Make-Ahead:** This parfait is great for meal prep. Prepare the chia pudding and berries the night before, and assemble the parfaits in the morning for a quick and easy breakfast.

This Chia Seed and Berry Breakfast Parfait is a tasty and nutritious option that provides a good balance of protein, fiber, and healthy fats. Enjoy this refreshing breakfast to kick-start your day!

Spiced Pumpkin Oatmeal

Ingredients:

- **1 cup rolled oats**
- **1 1/2 cups milk** (dairy or non-dairy, like almond milk)
- **1/2 cup canned pumpkin** (pure pumpkin, not pumpkin pie filling)
- **1/4 cup maple syrup** or honey (for sweetness)
- **1/2 tsp ground cinnamon**
- **1/4 tsp ground nutmeg**
- **1/4 tsp ground ginger**
- **Pinch of ground cloves** (optional)
- **1/4 tsp vanilla extract** (optional)
- **A pinch of salt**
- **Chopped nuts** or **seeds** for topping (optional, e.g., pecans, walnuts, or pumpkin seeds)
- **Fresh fruit** or **dried fruit** for topping (optional, e.g., apple slices or raisins)

Instructions:

1. **Cook the Oats:**
   - In a medium saucepan, combine the rolled oats, milk, and a pinch of salt. Bring to a boil over medium-high heat.
2. **Add Pumpkin and Spices:**
   - Reduce the heat to low and stir in the canned pumpkin, maple syrup (or honey), ground cinnamon, ground nutmeg, ground ginger, and ground cloves (if using).
3. **Simmer:**
   - Simmer the mixture, stirring occasionally, for about 5-7 minutes, or until the oats are cooked and the mixture is creamy. If the oatmeal is too thick, you can add a bit more milk to reach your desired consistency.
4. **Add Vanilla:**
   - Stir in the vanilla extract (if using) and cook for an additional minute.
5. **Serve:**
   - Spoon the oatmeal into bowls and top with your choice of toppings, such as chopped nuts, seeds, or fresh/dried fruit.

Tips:

- **Sweetness:** Adjust the sweetness to your taste. You can add more maple syrup or honey if you like your oatmeal sweeter.
- **Texture:** For a creamier texture, use full-fat milk or a non-dairy milk alternative with added creaminess. You can also stir in a spoonful of Greek yogurt for extra richness.
- **Make-Ahead:** This oatmeal can be made ahead and stored in the refrigerator for up to 4 days. Reheat with a splash of milk to loosen it up before serving.

This Spiced Pumpkin Oatmeal is a nutritious and flavorful breakfast that will keep you full and satisfied. Enjoy the comforting flavors and warming spices!

Egg and Spinach Breakfast Quesadilla

Ingredients:

- **2 large eggs**
- **1 cup fresh spinach**, chopped
- **1/4 cup shredded cheese** (e.g., cheddar, mozzarella, or feta)
- **1 tbsp olive oil** or butter
- **1 large tortilla** (whole wheat or flour)
- **Salt and black pepper**, to taste
- **1/4 tsp garlic powder** (optional)
- **1/4 tsp onion powder** (optional)
- **Fresh herbs** (e.g., chives, cilantro) for garnish (optional)
- **Salsa** or **sour cream** for serving (optional)

Instructions:

1. **Prepare the Eggs:**
    - In a bowl, whisk the eggs with a pinch of salt, black pepper, garlic powder, and onion powder (if using).
2. **Cook the Spinach:**
    - Heat a non-stick skillet over medium heat and add a small amount of olive oil or butter.
    - Add the chopped spinach and cook for 1-2 minutes, or until wilted. Remove from the skillet and set aside.
3. **Scramble the Eggs:**
    - In the same skillet, add a bit more oil or butter if needed. Pour in the whisked eggs and cook, stirring occasionally, until they are just set but still slightly soft. Remove from heat and stir in the cooked spinach.
4. **Assemble the Quesadilla:**
    - Wipe the skillet clean and heat it over medium heat. Place the tortilla in the skillet.
    - Sprinkle half of the shredded cheese evenly over one half of the tortilla.
    - Spread the scrambled eggs and spinach mixture over the cheese.
    - Sprinkle the remaining cheese over the eggs and fold the tortilla in half to cover the filling.
5. **Cook the Quesadilla:**
    - Cook the quesadilla for 2-3 minutes on each side, or until the tortilla is golden brown and the cheese is melted. Press down gently with a spatula to ensure even cooking.
6. **Serve:**
    - Remove the quesadilla from the skillet and let it cool for a minute before cutting into wedges.

- Garnish with fresh herbs if desired and serve with salsa or sour cream on the side.

Tips:

- **Add-Ins:** Feel free to add other ingredients to the filling, such as diced tomatoes, bell peppers, onions, or cooked bacon or sausage for extra flavor and protein.
- **Cheese:** Experiment with different cheeses to find your favorite combination. A blend of cheeses can also add extra richness.
- **Make-Ahead:** You can prepare the egg and spinach mixture ahead of time and store it in the refrigerator. Assemble and cook the quesadilla when ready to eat.

This Egg and Spinach Breakfast Quesadilla is a tasty and convenient way to enjoy a balanced breakfast that's full of flavor and nutrition. Enjoy!

Berry Almond Quinoa Porridge

Ingredients:

- **1 cup quinoa**, rinsed
- **2 cups water** or **milk** (dairy or non-dairy)
- **1/2 cup fresh or frozen berries** (e.g., blueberries, raspberries, strawberries)
- **1/4 cup sliced almonds** (or chopped almonds)
- **1-2 tbsp honey** or maple syrup (optional, for added sweetness)
- **1/2 tsp vanilla extract** (optional)
- **1/2 tsp ground cinnamon** (optional)
- **Pinch of salt**
- **Fresh mint** or **additional berries** for garnish (optional)

Instructions:

1. **Cook the Quinoa:**
   - In a medium saucepan, combine the rinsed quinoa and water (or milk). Add a pinch of salt.
   - Bring to a boil over high heat. Reduce the heat to low, cover, and simmer for about 15 minutes, or until the quinoa is tender and the liquid is absorbed. Remove from heat and let it sit, covered, for 5 minutes. Fluff with a fork.
2. **Prepare the Berries:**
   - If using fresh berries, wash them thoroughly. If using frozen berries, thaw them slightly before adding.
3. **Flavor the Quinoa:**
   - Stir in the vanilla extract, ground cinnamon (if using), and honey or maple syrup (if using) into the cooked quinoa. Mix well.
4. **Assemble the Porridge:**
   - Divide the cooked quinoa among bowls. Top with the berries and sliced almonds.
   - Drizzle with additional honey or maple syrup if desired.
5. **Garnish and Serve:**
   - Garnish with fresh mint or additional berries if desired.
   - Serve warm.

Tips:

- **Berry Variations:** Feel free to use any berries you like, or even a mix of berries. If you don't have berries, you can substitute with other fruits such as apples or pears.
- **Sweetness:** Adjust the sweetness according to your taste. You can also use a sugar substitute if preferred.
- **Add-Ins:** Consider adding other toppings such as chia seeds, flaxseeds, or a dollop of Greek yogurt for extra nutrition and flavor.

Berry Almond Quinoa Porridge is a wholesome and versatile breakfast that provides a good balance of protein, fiber, and healthy fats. Enjoy this tasty and nourishing start to your day!

Whole Wheat Avocado and Egg Toast

Ingredients:

- **2 slices whole wheat bread**
- **1 ripe avocado**
- **2 large eggs**
- **1 tbsp olive oil** or **butter**
- **Salt and black pepper**, to taste
- **Red pepper flakes** or **hot sauce** (optional, for a bit of heat)
- **Lemon juice** (optional, for added flavor)
- **Fresh herbs** (e.g., parsley, chives) for garnish (optional)

Instructions:

1. **Toast the Bread:**
   - Toast the whole wheat bread slices to your desired level of crispiness. You can use a toaster or toast them under the broiler.
2. **Prepare the Avocado:**
   - While the bread is toasting, cut the avocado in half, remove the pit, and scoop the flesh into a bowl.
   - Mash the avocado with a fork until smooth. You can season it with a pinch of salt, black pepper, and a squeeze of lemon juice if desired.
3. **Cook the Eggs:**
   - Heat olive oil or butter in a non-stick skillet over medium heat.
   - Crack the eggs into the skillet and cook to your preferred doneness:
     - **Sunny-side up:** Cook without flipping until the whites are set but the yolks remain runny.
     - **Over-easy:** Cook on one side, then gently flip and cook briefly on the other side for a runny yolk.
     - **Poached or scrambled eggs** are also great options if you prefer.
4. **Assemble the Toast:**
   - Spread the mashed avocado evenly over the toasted bread slices.
   - Top each slice with a cooked egg.
5. **Season and Garnish:**
   - Season the eggs with additional salt, black pepper, and red pepper flakes or hot sauce if desired.
   - Garnish with fresh herbs if using.
6. **Serve:**
   - Serve the avocado and egg toast immediately while the bread is still warm and crispy.

Tips:

- **Avocado Ripe:** Make sure your avocado is ripe for the best creamy texture and flavor. If it's not ripe, you can speed up the ripening process by placing it in a brown paper bag with an apple or banana for a few days.
- **Variations:** Feel free to add other toppings or ingredients like sliced tomatoes, radishes, or a sprinkle of cheese for extra flavor.
- **Meal Prep:** You can prepare the avocado mash ahead of time and store it in an airtight container in the refrigerator for up to 24 hours. Just give it a quick stir before using.

Whole Wheat Avocado and Egg Toast is a nutritious and satisfying meal that's perfect for breakfast or a light lunch. Enjoy this tasty combination of creamy avocado and protein-packed eggs!

Spinach and Mushroom Breakfast Casserole

Ingredients:

- **1 tbsp olive oil** or butter
- **1 cup mushrooms**, sliced (e.g., cremini, button, or shiitake)
- **1 cup fresh spinach**, chopped
- **1 small onion**, diced (optional)
- **6 large eggs**
- **1/2 cup milk** (dairy or non-dairy)
- **1/2 cup shredded cheese** (e.g., cheddar, mozzarella, or feta)
- **1/2 tsp dried oregano** or **thyme**
- **1/4 tsp garlic powder** (optional)
- **Salt and black pepper**, to taste
- **1/4 cup grated Parmesan cheese** (optional, for topping)

Instructions:

1. **Preheat Oven:**
   - Preheat your oven to 375°F (190°C). Grease a 9x9-inch baking dish or a similar-sized casserole dish.
2. **Sauté Vegetables:**
   - In a skillet, heat the olive oil or butter over medium heat.
   - Add the diced onion (if using) and cook until translucent, about 3-4 minutes.
   - Add the sliced mushrooms and cook until they are tender and any moisture has evaporated, about 5-7 minutes.
   - Stir in the chopped spinach and cook for another 2-3 minutes, until wilted. Season with a pinch of salt and black pepper.
3. **Prepare Egg Mixture:**
   - In a large bowl, whisk together the eggs, milk, dried oregano or thyme, garlic powder (if using), and a pinch of salt and black pepper.
   - Stir in the shredded cheese.
4. **Combine Ingredients:**
   - Add the sautéed vegetable mixture to the egg mixture and stir until well combined.
5. **Pour into Dish:**
   - Pour the mixture into the prepared baking dish and spread it out evenly.
6. **Add Topping:**
   - Sprinkle the grated Parmesan cheese on top if using.
7. **Bake:**
   - Bake in the preheated oven for 25-30 minutes, or until the casserole is set in the center and the top is golden brown.
8. **Cool and Serve:**

- Let the casserole cool for a few minutes before slicing. Serve warm.

Tips:

- **Vegetable Variations:** Feel free to add other vegetables like bell peppers, tomatoes, or zucchini for additional flavor and nutrition.
- **Cheese Options:** You can use your favorite cheese or a blend for different flavor profiles. Feta cheese adds a nice tanginess if you prefer.
- **Make-Ahead:** You can prepare the casserole a day in advance and refrigerate it. Reheat it in the oven before serving.

This Spinach and Mushroom Breakfast Casserole is a versatile and hearty option that's easy to make and perfect for feeding a crowd. Enjoy!

Kiwi and Pineapple Chia Seed Pudding

Ingredients:

- **1/4 cup chia seeds**
- **1 cup coconut milk** (or any other milk of your choice, such as almond milk)
- **1-2 tbsp honey** or maple syrup (optional, for added sweetness)
- **1/2 tsp vanilla extract** (optional)
- **1/2 cup fresh pineapple**, diced
- **1-2 ripe kiwis**, peeled and sliced
- **Fresh mint** for garnish (optional)

Instructions:

1. **Prepare the Chia Seed Pudding:**
   - In a bowl or jar, combine the chia seeds with the coconut milk. Stir well to ensure the chia seeds are evenly distributed and not clumping together.
   - Add honey or maple syrup if you prefer a sweeter pudding. Stir in the vanilla extract if using.
   - Cover and refrigerate for at least 4 hours or overnight. The chia seeds will absorb the liquid and turn into a pudding-like consistency. Stir occasionally to prevent clumping.
2. **Prepare the Fruit:**
   - While the chia pudding is setting, dice the fresh pineapple and slice the kiwis. Set aside.
3. **Assemble the Pudding:**
   - Once the chia pudding has set, give it a good stir. If it's too thick, you can add a little more milk to reach your desired consistency.
   - Spoon the chia pudding into serving glasses or bowls.
4. **Top with Fruit:**
   - Top the chia pudding with the diced pineapple and sliced kiwis.
5. **Garnish and Serve:**
   - Garnish with fresh mint leaves if desired.
   - Serve immediately or keep chilled until ready to serve.

Tips:

- **Fruit Variations:** Feel free to use other fruits like mango, strawberries, or berries if you prefer different flavors.
- **Sweetness:** Adjust the sweetness of the pudding according to your taste. You can add more honey or maple syrup if needed.
- **Make-Ahead:** Chia seed pudding is great for meal prep. Prepare it ahead of time and store it in the refrigerator for up to 4-5 days. Just add the fresh fruit before serving.

This Kiwi and Pineapple Chia Seed Pudding is a vibrant and tropical twist on the classic chia pudding, perfect for a refreshing breakfast or snack. Enjoy!

www.ingramcontent.com/pod-product-compliance
Lightning Source LLC
LaVergne TN
LVHW062048070526
838201LV00080B/2197